cook yourself thin

cook yourself thin

Harry Eastwood
Gizzi Erskine
Sal Henley
Sophie Michell

The delicious way to drop a dress size

an I**M**G media company

MICHAEL JOSEPH
an imprint of PENGUIN BOOKS

MICHAEL JOSEPH

Published by the Penguin Group
Penguin Books Ltd, 80 Strand, London WC2R 0RL, England
Penguin Group (USA) Inc., 375 Hudson Street, New York, New York 10014, USA
Penguin Group (Canada), 90 Eglinton Avenue East, Suite 700, Toronto, Ontario, Canada M4P 2Y3
(a division of Pearson Penguin Canada Inc.)
Penguin Ireland, 25 St Stephen's Green, Dublin 2, Ireland (a division of Penguin Books Ltd)
Penguin Group (Australia), 250 Camberwell Road,
Camberwell, Victoria 3124, Australia (a division of Pearson Australia Group Pty Ltd)
Penguin Books India Pvt Ltd, 11 Community Centre,
Panchsheel Park, New Delhi – 110 017, India
Penguin Group (NZ), 67 Apollo Drive, Rosedale, North Shore 0632, New Zealand
(a division of Pearson New Zealand Ltd)
Penguin Books (South Africa) (Pty) Ltd, 24 Sturdee Avenue,
Rosebank, Johannesburg 2196, South Africa

Penguin Books Ltd, Registered Offices: 80 Strand, London WC2R 0RL England

www.penguin.com

Published in 2007

2

Copyright © Tiger Aspect Productions Ltd, 2007
Recipes pages 72, 78, 79,81, 88, 98. 99. 111, 112, 132–3, 142–3, 148, 158, 160, 161, 172, 173, 183,
188, 194, 199, 200–201 copyright © Harry Eastwood, 2007
Recipes pages 71, 74, 77, 92, 93, 101, 104, 115, 119, 123, 134, 135–7, 150–51, 166–7, 168–9, 179,
181, 186, 187, 188, 196, 208, 211 copyright © Gizzi Erskine, 2007
Recipes pages 68, 80, 84, 87, 90, 94, 103, 110, 116, 124–5, 126–7, 140–41, 144, 154, 162–3, 178,
184, 189, 193, 202, 203, 210 copyright © Sal Henley, 2007
Recipes pages 70, 76, 85, 91, 95, 108, 118, 122, 128, 130–31, 138–9, 145–7, 157, 165, 175, 176, 182,
187, 198, 204, 208. 213 copyright © Sophie Michell, 2007
Nutritionist: Lynne Garton
Food stylist: Kim Morphew
Photography copyright © Yuki Sugiura, 2007
Additional photography on pages 7, 17, 21, 27, 33, 37, 43, 47, 49, 51, 59, 217 © Noel Murphy, 2007
Author portraits copyright © Colin Bell, 2007
Designed by Smith & Gilmour, London
Calligraphy by Peter Horridge

The moral right of the authors has been asserted

Printed in Great Britain by Butler & Tanner, Somerset

A CIP catalogue record for this book is available from the British Library

ISBN: 978–0–718–15351–9

Contents

Have your cake and eat it too!

This book will help you lose weight. But it's not a diet book. In fact, it's time to stop starving yourself and start loving food, because you really can shift the bulge and still indulge.

We are four normal women, just like you. We all work in the food industry and we *love* eating, but we're realistic enough to know that you can't eat anything and everything and expect to look hot in a bikini. We're busy people, not prepared to give up our social lives or our favourite treats to become slaves to a strict dietary regime. That's why we've used our expert knowledge to figure out the solutions, so you don't have to.

Among us, we've tried most of the diets out there – and failed. And we're not the only ones. One of the largest ever examinations of weight-loss studies found that up to two-thirds of dieters put on all the weight they lost within five years – and most end up heavier! No matter what the diet, the study found, it's unlikely to lead to lasting weight loss.

Sure, you will lose weight if you follow a diet to the letter. But how many of us can do that, and for how long? Most diet food tastes awful and the portions are minuscule, with the result that you fall off the wagon in spectacular style. Then follows the guilt, shame, feeling bad about yourself and almost inevitable overeating. It's no good for your body, mind or soul.

Yet still, we'll go to all sorts of lengths to feel thinner. Gizzi admits that portion control has never been in her vocabulary. Harry's subjected herself to grapefruit diets, patronizing Fat Fighters-style slimming clubs and years of yo-yo dieting. Sophie used to flit from feast to famine, never quite finding a happy balance, while it only took Sal one diet to realize that denial is the surest way to end up 'with your head in the chocolate drawer'.

Given this list of failures, you'd be forgiven for thinking we're on the flabby side. Not so. We're all very different heights and shapes and we're very happy with our figures, thank you, because we've finally learnt the secret to lasting weight loss. Today, we know quick fixes don't work and that there's only one simple way to lose weight without losing your mind: cook yourself thin.

We're not interested in denial or guilt . . .

Step away from the scales

The fact is, most of us don't need to revolutionize our eating habits; they just need a few tweaks. Dieticians and nutritionists agree that low-fat, low-calorie cooking skills, along with a basic knowledge of food labels and portion sizes, are the key to keeping trim. It has been suggested that consuming just 100 fewer calories every day (about a biscuit's worth) will prevent the average yearly weight gain of 2lb. That's not exactly starvation.

Another study showed most of us are used to eating just that little bit too much. It found women who consumed 800 calories a day less than normal felt just as full and satisfied. They did it by making *small* changes – for example, semi-skimmed milk instead of whole, half as much cheese, more vegetables, less fat. Small switches like these are easier to stick to and harder to go back on. But they add up to a significant drop in calories – and dress size.

Forget all or nothing, our approach is a positive attitude towards food. We're not interested in denial or guilt and we promise you mouthwatering temptation rather than any foods that remotely resemble cardboard. In this book, we'll show you how to quickly and easily figure out how and why you're consuming those few too many calories, then we'll share the secret to cutting down without missing out. We've taken up the challenge and done all our homework so we can make it easy for you. You don't have to become a culinary queen, you just need to cook more and cook *clever*.

We've tried, tested and tasted your favourite recipes and worked out all the cheats, tips, tricks and swaps you can use to make calories vanish into thin air. As foodies, we have really high standards, so you won't find any recipe or suggestion in this book that we're not convinced is better than the calorie-laden original. We all love a challenge and we've created recipes that use flavours and ingredients that will leave you in disbelief. All it takes is a little effort and you can learn to replicate your much-loved takeaways, comfort meals, snacks and desserts. And that's all there is to it: no sums, no weird foods or diet supplements, no denial, no sweaty exercise regime – just flavour, satisfaction and looser clothes. Happy cooking!

Harry, Gizzi, Sal and Sophie xxxx

Meet the Cook Yourself Thin team

Harry Eastwood

Harry's last supper

'Six snails and a chunk of really good baguette; a sirloin steak from an free-range, happy cow I've butchered myself, with proper French fries and Béarnaise sauce; some Vacherin cheese and a single chocolate truffle; all washed down with a couple of wowee wines. What a way to go!'

Harry was brought up in Qatar and France and has lived abroad for most of her life, being exposed to a colourful mix of cuisines. She loves 'getting her hands dirty' playing with food and inventing new dishes. For the past five years she's worked as a food stylist and writer, with a flair for sourcing the most beautiful ingredients at any time of the year and interpreting every recipe under the sun. She's cooked alongside amazing chefs as well as out of the back of vans.

Just to prove appearances can be deceptive, Harry is into pink, pearls, tiaras, all things pretty and, ah, butchery. That's right, she loves to prepare meat from field to plate so that she knows *exactly* where her dishes have come from and what's gone into them. Even though she spent four years as a vegetarian, there's now nothing Harry doesn't know about meat.

And forget fashion labels, Harry's into food labels – the higher quality the ingredients, the better. A free-range enthusiast, she'd rather retire than cook processed food. But censoring her ingredients is as far as food restrictions go. Her philosophy is that if you crave something it usually means your body (and soul) deserve it. She genuinely considers chocolate to be good for the soul and reckons it finishes a meal like a full stop finishes a sentence.

It'll come as no surprise, then, that Harry most definitely does not believe in restrictive diets. Food, she says, has been the joyful background to her life and learning to cook is the best weight-loss tool there is.

Gizzi Erskine

Gizzi spent much of her childhood in Thailand, which gave her a passion for the exotic from an early age. She loves Asian food, world ingredients and spice is her speciality, but she also favours comfort food in the form of slow, lovingly cooked stews and pies.

Portion control is not in Gizzi's vocabulary, nor is she prepared to go without, having tried and failed at a good few diets in her time. Instead, she believes staying in shape is all about balance – if you've overdone it one day, just cook yourself skinnier fare the next. And that's where her flair for flavour comes in handy. By using authentic ingredients, she creates vibrant Asian food that's naturally low in fat and ready in minutes.

After graduating from Leith's School of Food and Wine and beating off stiff competition to a training placement at *BBC Good Food* magazine, Gizzi went on to showcase her styling work in magazines, newspapers, books and for supermarkets, TV shows, films and advertising. Three years on, she is now in demand writing and styling recipes for the major glossies and has several celebrity clients ('but it's poor etiquette to name-drop, sorry!').

A vintage dresser and fashionista, Gizzi is a major music fan and gig-goer, always right on trend when it comes to the latest rock'n'roll bands. She likes to party as much as the next girl, but is just as much at home curled up on the sofa with her man, a mug of hot chocolate and a plate of shortbread.

Gizzi's last supper
'Tuna and sea bass sashimi to start; ponzu rock shrimps; crisp pork belly and coconut rice; followed by chocolate fondant and green tea ice cream.'

Sal Henley

Sal's last supper

'Mum's cooked breakfast made on the Aga; crispy aromatic duck with pancakes; home-made chocolate tart with vanilla ice cream; amazing cheeses and tons of alcohol – enough to poison me!'

If it's wholesome comfort food you're after, Sal's signature is 'traditional with a twist'.

Sal grew up on a hop farm in the Kent countryside where her family still cultivates fruit and livestock. A love of food is virtually in her genes and a career in the industry was a given by the time she took her first job with a local caterer. A food marketing degree and a stint at Leith's School of Food and Wine followed and for the past 10 years she's been a freelance food consultant and home economist.

A typical day might see Sal writing and testing recipes for magazines; food styling; giving cookery demonstrations or developing recipes and techniques for big industry clients. Her passion and enthusiasm once led to setting a wok alight in front of crowds at the BBC Good Food Show!

When she knocks off work, food is still a big feature of Sal's life. If she's not entertaining friends at home, she's dragging them off to the latest culinary hotspot to keep tabs on food trends.

Sal's favourite food includes an Oriental meal after a night on the town, a full English to put pay to hangovers and innovative roasts. Recently, she's made it her mission to develop versions of these dishes that hit the spot without hitting your hips. A passion for volleyball, skiing and outdoor pursuits also help keep her trim (as well as working up her endless appetite).

Sophie Michell

Sophie's favourite plaything at the age of 3 was her toy cooker; by 10 she was baking her own cakes and at 14 her professional kitchen career started. Her favourite books were cookbooks and her favourite pastime was eating good food ... and the same remains true today.

Sophie's passion for food and future cooking style was inspired by her eclectic upbringing and worldwide travels as a child. She studied at Butlers Wharf Chef School to obtain her advanced chef diploma, and then went on to work in some of the capital's best restaurants, including the Greenhouse, the Lanesborough, and the Embassy. At 19, she was nominated for the Young Chef of the Year award.

A passion for healthy eating led her to become family chef to a world-famous supermodel for 2 years and she's cooked for various VIP clients. Her first cookbook, *Irresistible,* was published in 2005.

Today, Sophie spreads her time across TV appearances, magazine and newspaper articles, supporting her favourite charities, menu consultancy and catering for fantastically glamorous events.

That is, of course, when she's not attending the fantastically glamorous events herself. Sophie's a self-confessed socialite and has a different date, dinner or party every night. She understands that every girl wants delicious, satisfying food, but also needs to fit into a sexy, slimline outfit and be out the door within the hour. So her recipes manage to be fast and fuss-free while still filling you up and tantalizing your taste buds.

ethos

What's your food personality?

Take our quick quiz to identify where the path of temptation lies for your taste buds. Combine this with the insights gleaned from your food diary, and you'll have your food personality nailed and know exactly where to cut calories for fast results. How easy is that?

A Quick Quiz

Try our quiz to find out your dieting downfalls. Pick the answer that most closely matches you.

What's in your fridge right now?
A. Half a bottle of Diet Coke (flat), some houmous and something unidentifiable with green stuff growing on it
B. A half-eaten giant slab of chocolate, a slice of lemon tart, Nutella
C. A packet of smoked salmon, some eggs, chilled bottle of vodka
D. Milk, cheese, leftover cottage pie

What would your desert-island dish be?
A. Thai green curry with rice
B. Devil's food cake
C. As I'd be by the sea, oysters and Champagne
D. A Sunday roast with all the trimmings

Which of these diets have you tried?
A. Low-fat
B. Every diet under the sun
C. No carbs
D. I've never dieted

Which of these dinner dates would you prefer?
A. Ordering in Chinese and cosying up on the sofa
B. An American-style ice-cream parlour
C. At the latest new restaurant in town
D. A pub lunch after a romantic walk in the country

When was the last time you ordered a takeaway?
A. About 12 hours ago
B. Ben & Jerry's don't do takeaway
C. When I had some friends around a couple of nights ago
D. Hardly ever – I'd rather cook it myself

And the last time you skipped a meal?
A. I rarely have breakfast but always eat at night, even if it's late
B. I sometimes skip straight to dessert
C. If I'm out, I usually miss dinner
D. When I was ill in 1997

Your favourite drink?
A. A grande latte
B. Hot chocolate with little marshmallows
C. Champagne, of course
D. A big mug of tea

You've been dumped. What do you do?
A. Get the girls round for DVDs and popcorn
B. Seek consolation from Cadbury's
C. Hit the town and flirt yourself better
D. Cook a big meal – it helps you de-stress

How does exercise figure in your life?
A. Running out the door to work
B. Hmm, exercise, yes I must get round to that
C. I'm a gym bunny – got to look good
D. I love walking and country hikes

Your vegetable of choice?
A. Do chips count?
B. Peas
C. Asparagus
D. Butternut squash

You and your kitchen – friend or foe?
A. It's a handy place to keep plates
B. We're friends that have grown apart
C. We don't spend much time together
D. Soul mates

What item sums up your kitchen?
A. An overflowing bin
B. My heart-shaped cookie cutters
C. A wok – for super-quick cooking before I go out
D. A giant casserole dish

What's the ideal way to finish a meal?
A. By going to bed
B. Pudding, of course
C. Dancing at my favourite club
D. A plate of cheeses

What would you cook to impress a new man?
A. I'd buy posh ready meals and hide the packets
B. Love me, love my tiramisu
C. As if! He'd be taking me out
D. Steak and chips and apple pie

What do you eat when you're starving?
A. A bag of crisps
B. I never get starving, I always keep chocolate handy
C. Canapés if I can spot any
D. Butter and Marmite on toast

What's your attitude towards dieting?
A. If I ate less junk I'd be OK, but I don't have time to cook
B. If it's banned, I want it more
C. If I've overdone it, I just eat less for a few days
D. Everything in moderation – but moderation's tough

How did you score?

Mostly As
You're a CONVENIENCE QUEEN.
You have the local Chinese, Indian and pizza place on speed dial. And they probably greet you like an old friend and know your order before you've uttered hello. Lunchtimes consist of whatever pre-packed sandwich the nearest eatery has to offer, and just about everything else you eat is munched on the run. We understand you're busy, but trust us, you'll feel a lot less frantic and stressed if you brave the kitchen once in a while. Cooking doesn't have to be complicated, as our recipes show. And you'll find that some of your favourite takeaway recipes can be created at a fraction of the cost, in the same amount of time it takes for them to be delivered, and – crucially – with nothing like the calories and fat you're currently consuming.

Mostly Bs
You're a SWEET-TOOTHED FAIRY.
You were born with a spoonful of sugar in your mouth. You'd happily forgo takeaways, ready meals and all other sorts of junk, so long as you didn't have to give up your daily sweet treats. There's always something chocolaty in your fridge, in the glove compartment of your car, in your handbag, on your desk at work – just in case. And if you can't finish a meal with something sweet, you almost feel panicked. Although you know you have a bit of an 'issue' with sugary foods, you feel powerless to resist it. Which is why we've worked out some super-rich quality treats that will give you that decadent high, without the guilt-ridden low. With a teensy bit of effort, you can have your cake and eat it.

Mostly Cs
You're a PARTY ANIMAL.
Appearance is important to you, so you do make more effort than most not to pig out at mealtimes. Problem is, your self-restraint is so good you often forgo meals altogether. Health aside, this ultimately has the effect of making your body think it's starving, so it'll hold onto any fat stores you have. Not a good idea. Time is also an issue for you. You often head out for drinks straight from work and unless food is on offer, you'll forget all about it and fill up on alcoholic empty calories. And boy is alcohol packed with calories. What, you didn't know that? We're not suggesting you stop socializing and stay in – heaven forbid! But try some of our cunning calorie swaps and super-fast meal ideas and you'll soon find fitting into your LBD is much less effort.

Mostly Ds
You're a COMFORT EATER.
You love food and home cooking. Some of your favourite recipes have been in your family for years, and just the smell of them makes you feel safe and happy. You're also a modern foodie and love nothing more than trying out the latest gastropub. You have a pretty good idea about nutrition and how to create a flavoursome, filling meal, but your enthusiasm for eating means portion control doesn't enter your mind – you'll have what he's having. Some of your cooking methods and ingredients are as antiquated as your recipes, too (it *is* possible to make tasty roast potatoes without lard, you know). Fortunately, while our recipes cut down on calories, they never compromise on taste or comfort. Open your mind to some new ingredients and techniques and you can feel cosy without looking cuddly.

So you want to drop a dress size?

Don't we all! Ask any woman on the street and the chances are she'd be happier if she could buy her jeans a size smaller, spare herself the discomfort of hold-it-all-in magic knickers, and shift that extra half stone she's been carrying since Christmas (that's Christmas 2003).

Contrary to media messages, we're not all hugely obese. Nor, thank heavens, size zero. The average dress size in the UK is 16. Only 25 per cent of women are classed as obese, but 32 per cent are overweight, so we do need to start watching what we eat. But despite the newspaper headlines, for most of us it's not about a total body transformation – we'd just like to get a little bit closer to our 'happy weight' and feel svelte and sexy.

It's a reasonable goal, so why does it seem so hard to achieve? Because, ladies, we're kidding ourselves. All too easily, we buy into the diet industry propaganda that tells us all our problems will be solved if we just cut out X or supplement with Y. We almost *want* to believe that weight-loss success comes only in the form of thimble-sized portions, eaten with children's cutlery. And when the inevitable happens and we fall off the diet wagon, we have the perfect excuse to dismiss weight loss as impossible and give up until next time.

The fact is, whether you think you're super-healthy and restrained or you acknowledge that your dietary halo needs a good polish, you – like all of us in the past – have probably been

That large latte and blueberry muffin you pop out for? 765 calories. Read it and weep . . .

deluding yourself. What you think of as an occasional habit may well have become a permanent fixture in your life. That large latte and blueberry muffin you pop out for most mornings around 11am? 765 calories, every day. Read it and weep. The bacon sandwich and can of Coke that never fails to cure your hangover? 540 calories. The Friday night curry meal? A whopping 1250 calories. Fine from time to time, but if these are a regular part of your diet, it's no wonder you think those skinny jeans have shrunk.

For Gizzi, it's all about the sweet stuff. She can't walk past one of those American doughnut shops without popping in to see what's on offer. OK as a treat, not so great as a regular habit. For Harry, a day's not worth living without chocolate.

You don't have to consume junk food around the clock to put on weight. There are certain foods that are just too darned yummy and tempting to resist, and the truth is you probably give in to them just a little more often than you admit to yourself. We can't resist them either, but we've learnt to cook or prepare many of them in a way that is far more delicious than the shop-bought options, with a fraction of the calories – and so can you.

All we require from you is a little effort in the kitchen and some good old-fashioned honesty. The bad news is we're going to ask you to keep a food diary for a week. But don't panic. This is not going to be one of those tedious, form-filling diets. This is the only time we're going to ask you to do anything like this.

So take a notebook, small and chic enough that you don't mind carrying it around with you all week. Ditto a stylish pen. Allow a couple of pages per day and write the name of the day at the top of the appropriate page. Then, from the moment you wake to the moment you hit the pillow at night, record every morsel of food or sip of drink that passes your lips. At the risk of being pedantic, we can't emphasize this point enough because, more often than not, it's our more unconscious habits that get us into trouble. So that handful of tortilla chips at a drinks party, the tiny slice of cake you have for a colleague's birthday celebration in the office, the little pieces of cheese you slice off every time you go to the fridge – they all count because the devil's in the details.

Be prepared to finish up with really long lists every day. This is normal. To help you get started, here's one we prepared earlier:

AM
Glass of orange juice
Black coffee
2 slices of thick white toast with butter
Banana
Large latte with a shot of syrup
Half a bag of fruit gums
PM
Chicken burger in a bun with mayo, salad with French dressing, chips and ketchup
2 cups of tea, semi-skimmed milk, 1 sugar
2 digestive biscuits
3 small chocolates from a selection box
EVENING
Half a large bag of tortilla chips
Half a pot of houmous
Supermarket own-brand diet fish pie ready meal
2 glasses of white wine
Cup of peppermint tea
Pot of diet strawberry mousse
Chocolate-chip cookie

The first step to changing your diet habits is to see exactly what you're currently eating on a day-to-day basis.

One Bourbon biscuit contains 67 calories while a handful of strawberries is only 7 calories.

When your diary is complete, give yourself half an hour to sit down and analyse it. Remember, this isn't an exercise in feeling bad about yourself. On the contrary, it's empowering. It's the perfect way to identify what your tastes and personal must-haves are when it comes to food and how to make sure you still satisfy that culinary lust as you shrink in size.

There's no magic scientific formula for the analysis – but a few different-coloured highlighter pens might come in handy. We just want you to scan your lists for patterns. These might be easy to spot (half a tub of ice cream, 9pm weekdays) or less obvious (like the fact you eat more when you're cooking for your man). Make a note of anything that occurs to you. It might be useful to highlight these and then add up the following:

Any foods or drinks that crop up
   every day or more
All alcoholic drinks
All non-diet fizzy drinks
All food bought and consumed on the
   run (such as a lunchtime sandwich)
All takeaway meals
All meals out
Sweet snacks
Savoury snacks
Blow outs

Hopefully, you'll see one or two patterns emerge from this process. You might discover that you tend to 'graze' all day long, which can be perfectly fine if that means fruit for snacks and small portions at mealtimes, but start adding hunks of cheese and endless bags of crisps to three average meals per day and you can quickly see why the calories might be adding up. Or perhaps you've got into the habit of grabbing a chocolate bar every day at the same time. It's a pick-me-up you now feel you couldn't do without, but once you try Harry's Chocolate Truffles (page 199), you'll never look back. Many people eat pretty well during the week and then blow it all at the weekend on rather too many glasses of wine, takeaways and mountainous cooked breakfasts, while others are happy to spend time cooking wholesome meals at the weekend, but can't seem to find the time during the week. In the next few pages you'll pick up plenty of tips and tricks to help you pinpoint the easy changes you can make to cut your calories and start seeing the pounds drop off.

A quick guide to calories

If you're female and you made it as far as your mid-teens without using the word 'calorie', congratulations! There can't be many body-conscious women out there who aren't familiar with the term. But do we really know what it means? Time for a quick masterclass.

A calorie (or kilocalorie, same difference) is basically a unit that measures how much energy your body is able to get from food. Different nutrients in food provide different amounts of calories: for example, fat gives you about 9 calories per gram, alcohol 7, while carbohydrates and protein yield about 4.

To find out how many calories a food contains, you can either consult our Calorie Guide (page 216) or check the nutritional information on the food label if it comes packaged. Next to the word 'Energy' you'll find the calorie count in kcal (the common abbreviation for calories). Remember to check the *amount* of food this refers to though. Most labels show nutritional information for 100g of the product. If the packet weighs 200g and you intend to eat the lot, you'll need to double the calories. If it only weighs 50g, you can happily halve it.

Nutritional information
Typical values per 100g

Energy 245kj/58kcal

Protein 4.6g

Carbohydrate 7.2g
of which sugars 6.5g

Fat 1.2g
of which saturates 0.2g

Fibre 0.2g

Sodium 0.1g

An individual pork pie can contain more than 500 calories!

Just to confuse matters, food energy is also measured in kilojoules, and manufacturers often put the kilojoules (kj) figure on the food label right next to the kcal. Don't get them confused, or you'll think you're eating far more calories than you actually are – there are 4.186kj in 1kcal.

Keep an eye out for fat content too – particularly saturated. Anything over 3g of fat per 100g of food or 1.5g per 100ml liquid can't be classed as low fat. Over 20g and warning bells should go off. Health professionals say we shouldn't consume more than 70g fat in total a day. Remember, fat is packed with calories.

The UK Department of Health Estimated Average Requirements (EAR) are a daily calorie intake of 1940 calories per day for women and 2550 for men. Of course, this will vary according to your size and how active you are, but it's a good guide. Tot up your food diary figures and you may find you meet this or perhaps consume less on some days, while on others you eat enough for three of you. But contrary to the ideas behind many of the starvation diets we've all tried, losing weight doesn't mean existing on a few hundred calories a day. Here's a better way to think about it.

Each pound of body fat you carry has an energy content of 3,500 calories. So if you wanted to lose 1lb a week say (the amount most experts say is realistic and safe), you'd need to cut your calorie intake by 500 calories a day (500 x 7 days = 3,500). Take a look at your food diary and see how many calories some of your 'big offenders' contain and you'll see that cutting 500 a day is easier than you think. Add a little calorie-burning exercise (see page 62) and you'll be shedding pounds before you can say, 'Wow, that was easy'.

Buyer beware
Try not to get too excited if food packaging screams at you from the shelves that it's 'low fat', 'lite', 'reduced sugar' or one of the many other 'buy-me-I'll-make-you-thin' type promises. When a product boasts it's 90 per cent fat free, what that means is it contains 10 per cent fat, which is hardly negligible. And remember that 'low fat' doesn't mean 'low sugar', i.e. low in calories. If a pudding says it's 'reduced sugar', do you know how much sugar was in the original version? If the answer is enough to make your teeth fall out, chances are the reduced version is pretty calorific, too. The simple solution to all this confusion is, of course, to reject processed foods as much as possible – definitely steer clear of 'diet' foods – and get into the kitchen instead. And before you start protesting that you don't have the time, just think how long it takes to decipher a food label!

The big offenders

You know they're supposed to be occasional treats and they're hardly going to make you slim, but somehow you just can't resist them. Here we name and shame some of the biggest offenders when it comes to a calorie count. The good news is you don't have to give these up if you simply cook them our way.

Bar of milk chocolate 260 calories/50g bar
Chocolate digestive biscuit 85 calories
Can of cola 135 calories
Chicken biryani with rice (450g pack), 1 naan, 1 tbsp mango chutney and 2 poppadums 1250 calories
Restaurant-style Crispy Chicken Caesar salad 530 calories
Fried chicken wings in breadcrumbs 400 calories/2 wings
Chip-shop cod in batter with chips 950 calories
Slice of chocolate fudge cake 350 calories
Large, sharing packet of 'designer' crisps 240 calories/50g serving
1 croissant with butter and jam 345 calories
A full English (1 rasher of bacon, 2 sausages, 1 egg, black pudding, beans, 1 slice of bread – all fried) 1050 calories
Tall latte with whole milk 200 calories
Meat-feast pizza 250 calories/100g
Quarter pounder burger with cheese 515 calories
Shepherd's pie 350 calories
Spaghetti carbonara 600 calories/400g serving
Sweet-and-sour pork with egg-fried rice 760 calories
Tiramisu 260 calories
Half a tub of vanilla premium ice cream 460 calories/250ml
White double chocolate chip muffin 300 calories

(Calorie counts based on average portion sizes and ingredients, these can vary a great deal depending on the brand.)

The surprise offenders

Generally, we know when we're indulging. As you close your eyes and savour that first bite of rich, creamy lemon tart, you know you're not fooling anyone, least of all yourself. It's a decadent thrill that tastes all the better for being naughty. But what about those everyday foods that look so innocent?

> The trouble with so-called diet brands is they often taste bland and don't fill you up – leading to the dreaded snack attack later.

Sometimes, despite our most virtuous intentions, the calories just slip past our radar. You think you're munching away on a super-healthy snack when you might just as well have had a Danish pastry and be done with it.

Some savoury foods contain surprising amounts of sugar. Likewise, products that boast they're 'low fat' often compensate by being high in sugar. Don't let foods like these fool you with their healthy façade. However, we're not saying they're *bad* for you and you should give them up – far from it. A fruit smoothie is a great way to get your vits and olive oil has countless beauty and health benefits. But it's worth noting their surprising calorie count if these items figure more than two or three times in your food diary.

It's sugar, but not as you know it
Food manufacturers have canny ways of concealing a food's sugar content from us, one being that they'll list different types of sugars separately.

Check the label for:
Corn syrup
Dextrose
Fructose
Fruit sugar
Glucose
Golden syrup
High fructose corn/glucose syrup
Hydrolysed starch
Invert sugar
Lactose
Levulose
Maltose
Milk sugar
Molasses
Sucrose
Treacle

Alcohol – fun but full of empty calories, especially if it's dark or sweet

Cereal – sugary cereals tend to be higher in calories than high-fibre cereals and far less satisfying

Cereal bars – they may look healthy, but check the label

Frozen chips – watch out for those coated in calorific seasoning

Nuts – full of vitamins and minerals, but don't overdo it. Choose raw over roasted

'Good' oils – a dietary essential, just watch how much you slosh on

Peanut butter – good for you, but spread it thin

Cinema popcorn – smuggle in your own for a fraction of the cals and price

Pre-packed sandwiches – the fillings can be swimming in fatty sauces

Shop-bought or restaurant salads – dressings, croutons, fatty meat and cheese can turn a light lunch into a calorie-laden pig out

Fruit smoothies – go for fruity rather than yoghurty and check for added sugars

Soups – check for hidden sugar and cream, and even better if you make your own (see pages 106–19)

Fruit squash/cordial – 'posh' drinks like elderflower sound healthy, but are just as sugary as kids' drinks

Toast with butter – easy to OD on butter as it melts into the bread.

Veggie burger – extra fat is often used to boost flavour

Yoghurts – sound healthy and often are, but some are high in fat and sugar. Check before you buy

Ingredients for success

One of the main excuses we hear for cobwebs in the kitchen is lack of time: 'I don't get in from work till late and there's no point cooking'. 'A takeaway is quicker and easier when I'm tired.' 'There's never any food in the house.' 'I'm too busy to do a weekly shop.'

Stock up on good things to eat, healthy snacks and a week's worth of meals. Add a couple of new ingredients each time to experiment with. After all, we all love shopping!

Believe it or not, we can empathize. We often work long days cooking, on TV or magazine shoots and when we fall through the door late in the evening, the last thing any of us want to do is slave over a hot stove (again). We even understand the 'nothing in the fridge' excuse – supermarkets can be stressful places.

But if you're serious about putting a dent in your calorie quota, a takeaway or ready meal is not the answer. There are plenty of great-tasting but skinny meals you can make in minutes. The key is having a well-stocked storecupboard. One trip to the shops, armed with the list below, is all it takes (or even a click of the mouse if you shop online). You don't need to buy it all in one go, but these are the sort of items you'll wonder how you coped without.

The following list is made up of cooking basics, condiments, herbs and spices, all of which form the basis for some really easy, yummy dishes. Sal's favourite use for storecupboard ingredients, for example, is a risotto made from just garlic, onion, olive oil, arborio rice, chicken stock and Parmesan. You could add other ingredients if you had them, such as mushrooms, asparagus or prawns, but even as a stand-alone dish, this looks and tastes impressive.

Some of the meals you can knock together from this list are so basic they don't need recipes. And we hope you'll soon start to create your own, too.

We've also included a few of our favourite foodstuffs to have in the fridge. Obviously, you'll still want to swing by the shops from time to time to pick up your fresh fruit and veg, meat, fish and dairy. So we recommend you also grab these goodies each time you go.

With your newly stocked cupboards, you'll never use the 'nothing to eat' excuse again.

Basics

Couscous – ultra quick and easy food. Just pour over boiling water and leave to absorb

Eggs – the ultimate fast food, super filling and versatile ingredient

Garlic

Lemons – perfect salad dressing sauce/sauce ingredient

Limes

Meringue nests – just add berries and some 0% fat Greek yoghurt and you have miniature pavlova portions that deserve a low-cal prize

Oatcakes

Oats – for porridge, cereal bars, flapjacks, crumble toppings

Onions

Pasta

Popping corn – a brilliant low-cal snack. Only when you add butter or sugar do you need to be wary

Pumpkin seeds – great in salads. Rumour has it they're an aphrodisiac, too!

Rice (brown, brown basmati, Thai and arborio)

Rice noodles (brown) – ready in seconds

Sunflower seeds

Herbs and spices

Basil – keep a fresh pot on your windowsill if possible

Bay leaves

Black peppercorns

Coriander – fresh if possible

Coriander seeds

Cumin seeds

Dried chilli flakes – use sparingly, but saves chopping fresh chillies

Fennel seeds

Mint – fresh if possible

Nutmeg

Oregano – dried is best for a more intense flavour

Paprika

Parsley – fresh and flat-leaf

Sage – fresh or dried

Thyme – dried is fine

Adding flavour through herbs and spices is an easy route to low-calorie cooking with no compromise on taste.

Condiments

Aged balsamic vinegar – a fat-free dressing or dip

Capers

Chicken and beef stock concentrate (from your butcher) – this lasts for ages and makes amazing gravies and soups. Harry swears it's worlds apart from any stock cube

Cocoa

Cornflour – for thickening sauces and gravy

Dried porcini mushrooms

Extra-virgin olive oil – buy the best quality you can; the denser the flavour, the less you'll use

Fructose – a sugar substitute. Use about a fifth less than you would of sugar

Gherkins – as a snack, but they also add piquancy sliced onto a pizza, pasta and fish

Clear honey – the most neutral-flavoured, versatile honey, good for adding sweetness

Japanese sesame and seaweed seasoning – sprinkle over rice and stir-fries for flavour, colour and bite. Makes a good crust for salmon

Maldon sea salt crystals

Maple syrup

Marigold vegetable bouillon – a flavoursome stock powder

Marmite

Miso paste – just add boiling water for instant miso soup. An easy way to jazz up steamed veg

Mustards (Dijon, English, wholegrain) – for salad dressings, glazes and sandwiches

Olives

Oyster sauce – low-cal, low-fat stir-fry sauce and delicious over green veg or on an omelette with spring onions

Red wine vinegar

Rice wine vinegar

Soy sauce – not just for Asian cooking, it also adds depth and colour to gravies and sauces. Mix soy, lime, chilli flakes, garlic and coriander for an impressive dip. Or just drizzle over Thai rice

Sundried tomatoes

Sweet chilli sauce – Sophie's almost addicted to this. Perfect for dipping or brushed over prawns before griddling

Tabasco – like dried chilli powder, this adds heat to food when you're out of fresh chillies or don't want to risk rubbing your eyes after chopping one (ow!)

Tahini – sesame seed paste. Good on rye bread, veg or use to make houmous

Thai fish sauce – OK, it smells *awful*, but trust us, it tastes nothing like that. Once you start using this to add that extra something to dishes, you won't know how you coped without it

Vanilla beans – Sal's favourite pudding ingredient, the seeds transform something simple like fruit and yoghurt into something special

Wasabi – because some like it *hot* (try it mixed with horseradish to raise hell at next Sunday's roast)

White wine vinegar

Worcestershire sauce – creates a flavour explosion in meaty dishes

Xylitol – a natural sweetener that contains 40 per cent fewer calories than refined white sugar

Mix soy, lime, chilli flakes, garlic and coriander for an impressive dip. Or just drizzle over Thai rice

Fridge and freezer favourites

Bread (pittas, flour tortillas and granary) – for the freezer

Cheddar – the stronger in flavour the cheese, the less you'll want to use

Block of hard goat's cheese – handy for slicing off into salads or on pizza. 'Love the stuff', says Harry

Dark chocolate – at least 70% cocoa solids

Frozen fruit and vegetables – such as peas, broad beans, sweetcorn and summer fruits

Parmesan – *never* the pre-grated type! Do it yourself and you'll eat less, especially if you use a microplane grater (see page 44)

Peanut butter – used sparingly, this is a healthy source of protein. Makes a filling snack on rye bread or oatcakes

Prosciutto or Parma ham

Tofu (solid, not silken) – a low-fat protein, great to slice into cubes for last-minute salads and stir-fries

Half-size bottles of wine or Champagne – a whole open bottle sometimes means that you just finish it!

0% fat Greek yoghurt – one of the few fat-free versions of a product that really works. You can use this as a substitute for cream, crème fraîche, mayo or wherever you need something creamy

Tins

Anchovies – absolutely brilliant for adding flavour. Try these (even if you don't think you like them) forked into a paste to add saltiness and depth to dressings, dips and sauces

Beans (black eye, borlotti, butter) – a quick, low fat and easy source of protein to make salads, stews and fajitas more filling

Chickpeas – add to salads and couscous or whiz up with tahini, garlic, olive oil, lemon juice and cumin to make houmous

Salmon – all tinned fish is handy for a quick salad or to mould into fishcakes

Sardines

Tomatoes – a must-have for speedy pasta sauces

Tuna in spring water

Kitchen equipment

Good, fast, fuss-free cooking is all about the equipment you use. You don't have to spend a fortune or clutter your work surfaces with electrical items – we're talking about a few choice pieces that will make your food skinnier and your life easier. Here are the items we can't live without.

Beautiful plates – what's the point of great-looking food on nasty, chipped plates?

Blender – you won't need this and a food processor and a handheld blender unless you're a really keen cook (with a big kitchen), but a countertop blender is great if you often make smoothies and soups in big quantities. A glass jug is a better investment than plastic. Comes in handy for cocktails, too!

Handheld blender – this is handy for smaller quantities, such as making a soup or smoothie for one or two. It's portable, doesn't take up much room and is easy to clean. Sophie loves hers

Handheld electric whisk – like a handheld blender, this is portable, easy-clean and saves aching arms if you're whisking egg whites or making a cake

Food processor – if you have room, leave this out on your kitchen top permanently and you'll use it more often. Once you realize what a time- and labour-saver this is, you'll fall in love. As well as blending, liquidizing and whisking, you'll use it for cakes, making breadcrumbs, whizzing up toppings, pâtés and pastes

Ridged griddle or grilling pan – for chargrilling meat, fish and veg. This is low- or no-fat fast cooking with an extra smoky flavour. Those barbecue-style griddle marks make you feel like summer's with you all year round

Empty jars – one of Harry's favourite tips, perfect for taking soups and smoothies to work

Kitchen paper – for blotting grease off food after cooking

Measuring jug and spoons

Metal tongs – the easiest way to turn food on the grill or in the pan and transfer to plates

Microplane grater – Gizzi's kitchen must-have, this makes lightning-quick work of citrus zest, ginger, garlic and cheese. A little goes a long way so you'll cut down on the amount of cheese you use without noticing

Good-quality pans – two or three saucepans with thick, sturdy bases, tall sides, stay-cool handles and well-fitting lids; a large, heavy-based, non-stick sauté pan that can be used for searing/flash-frying; and a casserole dish. Stainless steel looks stylish, is hard wearing and easy to clean

Omelette pan – perfect for quick meals for one or for toasting nuts. Buy non-stick and you won't need oil

Pastry brush – for lightly oiling food before cooking

Pepper grinder

Pestle and mortar – the quickest way to make spice mixes and pesto. Use fresh spices for flamboyant flavours and you'll never notice the lack of fat. Buy a large stone one if you can – smaller porcelain ones are fiddly

What's the point of great-looking food on nasty, chipped plates?

Plastic containers – you'll need airtight ones for storing leftovers or for when you're super-organized and make food in batches to freeze for future meals

Non-stick roasting tray – buy one with a sturdy base that can also go on the hob

Scales – forget silly diet scales, we're not trying to enforce strict portion control. You just need a decent set to weigh out ingredients

Sharp knives – even just one super-sharp, high-quality knife is an investment you won't regret

Spatula – Harry's favourite kitchen tool (hers has little hearts all over it)

Steamer – An absolute kitchen essential. Some saucepans come with a steamer that fits on top or you can buy a universal steaming basket that fits into the pan

Large wok with a lid – if you look after your wok and season it after every use, you'll hardly need any oil. Sal points out that most people's wok lids are gathering dust, but they're useful for steaming veg

Wooden chopping board – longer lasting than plastic

Wooden spoons

And the white elephants of the kitchen?
If you have any of the following, save space by donating them to a jumble sale. Life's too short to use a:

Blunt knife
Deep-fat fryer
Egg poacher
Electric citrus press
Pasta maker
Pressure cooker
Salad spinner
Sandwich toaster
Yoghurt maker

Where did all the calories go?

Now you've invested in the right equipment, you're ready to get cooking. As well as choosing lower-calorie foods, what you do with them can make a real difference to your waistline. As you get to grips with our recipes over the following pages, you'll pick up lots of ideas for cooking without the fat or extra calories.

Instead of frying, grill or bake food or dry-fry using minimal oil in a non-stick pan.

Poaching in a liquid (such as water or stock) is fat-free and an excellent way of keeping meat and fish moist and full of flavour. A chicken breast, for example, tastes much more succulent poached in stock than roasted. You can do it on the hob or in the oven. Just cover the food in liquid, place a lid on the pan and cook for the same time you would roast, grill or fry.

Try halving the sugar in recipes (apart from ours, which are already low). It works for most dishes except jam, meringue and ice cream. Or use one of the sugar substitutes recommended on our list of storecupboard ingredients on page 34.

Steaming vegetables preserves more colour, flavour, nutrients and crunch than boiling. You can also use your steamer for fish and meat. If you have a stacking system, such as a bamboo steamer, put the veg that will take longest to cook at the bottom.

Buy lean cuts of meat and trim off excess fat before cooking – or ask your butcher to do it for you – and remove the skin from poultry.

Even if a recipe does call for some oil for roasting or frying, that doesn't mean all of it has to end up in the dish. You can drain off the fat at any point during cooking and transfer the food onto a wad of kitchen paper to blot it before serving.

If you need to prevent sticking, use a pastry brush to put the oil onto the food itself, *not* the pan, griddle or grill. This way you'll use much less.

When you chargrill meat on a griddle pan, a common mistake is too add more oil because you think it's stuck. Don't – the meat will release itself from the ridges once it's charred.

When stir-frying in a wok, you only need a tiny drizzle of oil to start with. Keep the food moving in the wok and the wok moving over the heat and nothing will stick. Then, to steam the food, add a splash of liquid such as water or soy sauce and put on the wok lid.

Most dishes that you think have to be fried are just as successful grilled or chargrilled in a non-stick griddle pan.

To save on washing-up and soul-destroying oven cleaning, line your grill pan and the bottom of your oven with foil to catch drips. You can even line roasting trays with a non-stick Teflon-coated sheet.

Comparative cooking methods
FILLET OF COD:
Deep fried in batter 445 calories
Pan fried in 2 tsp vegetable oil 150 calories
Grilled 96 calories
Steamed 96 calories
CHICKEN BREAST:
Chicken kiev ready-made 456 calories
Pan fried in 1 tsp butter and 1 tsp vegetable oil (no skin) 202 calories
Brushed with 1 tsp honey and grilled (no skin) 161 calories
Oven-baked in a foil pocket with chicken stock and a dash of white wine 151 calories

Cunning calorie swaps

Sometimes you just don't have time to stop and do the maths before you indulge. So here, we've done the hard work for you and calculated some simple but brilliant switches you can make for huge calorie savings – with no compromise on taste.

Breakfasts

We're all fans of big breakfasts. Believe it or not, if you set yourself up well from the start, it gets your metabolism going so you'll burn more calories during the day. Skip breakfast, on the other hand, and come 11am you'll be heading out the door on a muffin run, no question. It pays to choose wisely though. The following delicious swaps mean you'll miss out on nothing but calories.

SWAP FOR

Two thick slices of toast with butter and chocolate spread (630 calories) / Two medium slices of toast with butter and marmite (335 calories)

Croissant with butter and jam (345 calories) / Brioche roll, no butter (205 calories)

Three rashers of fried bacon in a white bap with butter (545 calories) / Two rashers of grilled bacon with tomato on one slice of wholemeal toast, no butter (235 calories)

Full English: bacon, sausage, tomato, mushrooms, beans, egg, black pudding, fried bread (1050 calories) / Skinnier Cooked Breakfast, page 74 (472 calories)

Cornflakes with whole milk and two teaspoons of sugar (218 calories) / Cornflakes with skimmed milk and half a banana (185 calories)

Two fried eggs on two slices of buttered toast (545 calories) / Poached egg on rye, no butter (135 calories)

Eggs Benedict (300 calories) / Two slices of smoked salmon and scrambled egg (made with semi skimmed milk and no butter) (220 calories)

Lunches and snacks

Admittedly, it's very hard to find decent fare when you're on the go. High-street cafés and chains in stations and shopping centres normally rely on fat to add flavour and disguise poor-quality food. Likewise, those convenience snacks you grab for a Friday night in with the girls aren't so convenient calorie-wise. But we've done the maths and worked out a few handy swaps for you.

SWAP FOR

Large jacket potato with butter and tuna mayo (770 calories) / Medium jacket potato with reduced-fat houmous and chargrilled Mediterranean veg (515 calories)

Large jacket potato with butter, beans and cheese (650 calories) / Chicken and Mushroom Risotto Soup, page 115 (332 calories)

Packet of 'designer' salted crisps (240 calories/ 50g serving) / Two oatcakes with low-fat soft cheese (40 calories)

BLT sandwich on malted bread 540 calories) / Tuna Niçoise Wrap, page 101 (305 calories)

Tuna and cheese melted panini (600 calories) / Takeaway sushi tray (250 calories)

Cheese ploughman's with bread, butter, Cheddar and pickle (700 calories) / Tricolour salad with mozzarella, avocado and tomato (500 calories)

Packet (50g) of roasted salted peanuts (300 calories) / Large handful (285g) of mixed dried fruit (67 calories)

Cream of tomato soup (155 calories) / Tomato, Chilli and Basil Soup, page 108 (95 calories)

Handful (28g) of roasted salted cashews (155 calories) / Handful (25g) of mini pretzels (95 calories)

Tortilla chips and sour cream dip (320 calories) / 4 Breadsticks and tzatziki (100 calories)

Takeaways and fast food

If you've simply got to have it (and there's nothing wrong with that), check the menu before you blurt out your standard order. With a few cunning choices, takeaways needn't be so terrible after all. Better still, cook your own skinny versions with our recipes – so easy they'll be on your plate before the pizza man's knocked on the door.

SWAP FOR

Half a pepperoni pizza (545 calories) / Pepperoni and Parmesan Pitta Pizzas, page 94 (287 calories)

One slice of Hawaiian-style deep pan pizza (275kcal) / One slice of Hawaiian style thin crust pizza (245kcal)

Regular skinny fries (325 calories) / 100g Chunky potato wedges (150 calories)

Large quarterpounder cheeseburger with cheese and bacon in bun (590 calories) / Mexican burgers, page (456 calories)

Crispy chicken Caesar salad with dressing and croutons (530 calories) / Chicken Caesar Salad with Melba Toasts, page 92 (372 calories)

Chicken tikka masala with pilau rice and half a naan (1055kcal calories) / Chicken Tikka Masala with Fragrant Rice, page 135 (256 calories)

Sweet-and-sour pork with egg-fried rice (760 calories) / Chicken and Prawn Egg-fried Rice, page 140 (402 calories)

Chicken satay with peanut sauce and fried rice (775 calories) / Chicken chow mein (515 calories)

Chip-shop cod in batter and large chips (950 calories) / Fish and Chips with Mushy Peas, page 126 (403 calories)

Lamb kebab with mayo and chips (975 calories) / Lebanese Chicken Kebabs with Garlic Sauce and Pickles, page 134 (365 calories)

Sweet treats

Friends always asking you how you eat so much sugary stuff and still stay slim? Tell them it's our little secret. These sweet cheats are our finest achievement to date.

SWAP FOR

Bar of chocolate (260 calories) / Two Chocolate Truffles, page 199 (106 calories)

Coffee-shop blueberry muffin (500 calories) / Two slices of fruit bread, no butter (180 calories)

Coffee-shop cinnamon-and-raisin Danish (410 calories) / Currant bun, no butter (170 calories)

Chocolate chip-and-nut shortbread cookie biscuit (105 calories) / Jaffa cake (45 calories)

Slice of strawberry cheesecake (275 calories) / One meringue nest with strawberries and 0% fat Greek yoghurt (105 calories)

Two scoops of dairy ice cream 210 calories) / Two scoops of frozen yoghurt (150 calories)

Banoffee pie (440 calories) / Banoffee Pie Pots, page 196 (289 calories)

Slice of lemon meringue pie 240 calories) / Lemon Meringue Mess, page 194 (266 calories)

Bread-and-butter pudding and custard made with whole milk (415 calories) / Chocolate and Orange Tiramisu, page 195 (217 calories)

Coffee-shop chocolate brownie (275 calories) / 30g melted dark chocolate with pear dipping slices (215 calories)

Drinks

Reducing your calorie intake isn't just about the food you eat. Many soft drinks contain the same amount of calories as a decent snack, yet research proves people don't get the same satisfaction from drinks as they do from food. A recent US study found Americans get 22 per cent of their daily calories from soft drinks and half the added sugar they consume comes in liquid form. We may not quite have their thirst for 'Big Gulp' beverages, but it pays to get savvy because, for many of us, swapping a daily high-cal drink for a low-cal one could add up to serious slimming success in no time at all.

SWAP FOR

Large coffee-shop latte (265 calories) / Small skinny latte (120 calories)

Can of Coke (135 calories) / Diet Coke (1 calorie)

Mug of hot chocolate with cream and marshmallows (360 calories) / Mug of cocoa made with skimmed milk (120 calories)

Large cappuccino with whole milk, 473ml (155 calories) / Filter coffee with semi-skimmed milk (15 calories)

Pint of orange juice and lemonade (165 calories) / Pint of grapefruit and soda (95 calories)

Glass of sparkling elderflower (75 calories) / Glass of sparkling water with squeeze of lime (0 calories)

Mug of tea with whole milk and two sugars (50 calories) / Mug of herbal tea (0 calories)

Bottle of strawberry-flavoured milkshake (190 calories) / Pink Smoothie, page 79 (97 calories)

Alcohol

If you're convinced you never overeat and don't understand why you can't shift that half stone, look to your bar bill. Alcohol is second only to fat in the amount of calories it provides and they're 'empty' calories – they won't fuel you or fill you up. There are many health risks associated with alcohol so the best tip is to consume in moderation and when you fancy a tipple, try our tips to save on the calories too.

SWAP FOR (all mixers 100ml, wine 120ml, spirits 25ml)

Vodka and cranberry juice (108 calories) / Vodka and tomato juice (67 calories)

Pina colada (593 calories) / Rum and pineapple juice (102 calories)

Mojito (242 calories) / Seabreeze (140 calories)

Baileys (175 calories) / Sambuca (103 calories)

Pint of lager (165 calories) / Glass dry white wine (77 calories)

Mulled wine (227 calories) / Glass red wine (80 calories)

Gin and tonic (120 calories) / Gin and slimline tonic (55 calories)

Margarita (145 calories) / Glass champagne (91 calories)

The skinny alternatives

We're not here to put you on a rigid plan – that might work for the duration of a diet but then where does it leave you at the end? More often than not, back to square one. The key with *Cook Yourself Thin* is to tweak your diet, not go on one, and make a few changes to create a lasting difference.

Convenience Queen

Blueberry muffin and a large latte from that well-known coffee shop around the corner
Swap for 2 slices of wholemeal toast (keep bread in the freezer for extra convenience) with butter and marmite and a filter coffee with a splash of milk to save a whopping 450 calories

BLT sandwich and a pressed apple juice
Swap 250ml pressed apple juice for an apple and save 60 calories

Early evening fridge raid – two thick slices of white bread and butter
That's nearly 400 calories – swap for your favourite fruit

Lasagne ready meal and salad ...and a bottle of beer
Make Sophie's lasagne, page 145, at the weekend and you can keep it chilled for up to three days. Save an average of 200 calories compared with supermarket versions. Swap the beer for fizzy water and you'll save another 100 calories

Sweet-Toothed Fairy

Honey nut cornflakes with whole milk
Swap for cornflakes, half a banana and semi-skimmed milk and you won't need those custard creams mid-morning

4 custard creams
These really are just an empty sugar hit and 236 calories – swap for a piece of fruit, a handful of cherries is 14 calories, and you'll get the same sweet hit

6 cups of tea with milk and 2 sugars throughout the day
These are clocking up 300 extra calories per day – if you can wean yourself off the sugar, you'll save 240 calories as quickly as you can say 'put the kettle on'

Chicken salad
Just watch out for heavy dressings

Can of fizzy orange
Swap for a diet version, or if you just hate diet drinks then grab an orange and save over 100 calories

Spinach and ricotta ravioli with herby tomato sauce
Good choice

Shop-bought chocolate cheesecake
Swap for one of Harry's amazing chocolate truffles, page 199, save up to 200 calories

Party Animal

Nothing for breakfast
This is a bad idea –
saving calories first
thing usually leads to
a need for sugary hits
later in the morning

Danish pastry and a
cappuccino mid-morning
See! Swap for a bowl
of muesli with semi-
skimmed milk and
an Americano to save
nearly 300 calories

Chicken Ceasar salad
Swap for Gizzi's slimline
version, page 92, and
save over 200 calories

After work – 3 glasses
of white wine, half a
plate of chips and mayo
Not much food for
nearly 600 calories.
Try alternating a glass
of wine with a Diet Coke
or sparkling mineral
water and have
something to eat
before you go out

Before bed – cheese
on toast x 2
Another 540 calories.
If you know you're going
to get home hungry,
keep some 5-minute
meals on hand, like miso
soup with noodles, or
heat up some soup you
made at the weekend

Comfort Eater

Bacon sandwich
with butter and
tomato ketchup
Swap for mushrooms
and one slice of bacon
on one slice of toast,
no butter, to save
380 calories

Cream of tomato soup
and 2 slices of toast
with butter and pate
Homemade tomato
soup, page 108, is
wonderful and if you
also swap the paté for
low-fat houmous you'll
save over 150 calories

Five Bourbon biscuits.
These very quickly
add up to 335 calories.
A small bowl of popcorn
(no butter or sugar) is
only 60 calories – the
perfect comfort snack

Macaroni cheese and
tomato salad. Macaroni
cheese can easily contain
over 800 calories . . . gulp!
Swap for Sal's Carbonara,
page 144, to save over
300 calories

Exercise

We're not suggesting you have to do exercise – merely that you might like to from time to time as a cunning way to earn yourself an extra calorie allowance. You might even be doing it without noticing – your walk to work, throwing shapes on the dancefloor, a night of passion … it all adds up.

The following activities all burn round about 100 calories. So next time you've overindulged, you can restore the balance in no time at all. Game of pool anyone?

Aerobics	20 minutes	100 calories
Cross trainer	15 minutes	90 calories
Cycling	15 minutes	93 calories
Dancing	25 minutes	112 calories
Gardening	25 minutes	95 calories
Jogging	15 minutes	90 calories
Netball	20 minutes	92 calories
Playing pool	30 minutes	99 calories
Sex	20 minutes	100 calories
Skiing	20 minutes	120 calories
Swimming (breaststroke)	10 minutes	91 calories
Tennis	15 minutes	108 calories
Walking	30 minutes	105 calories
Weight-training	40 minutes	96 calories
Yoga	40 minutes	104 calories

Sources: eatwell.gov.uk/healthy diet, Juliette Kellow's Calorie, Carb & Fat Bible 2007 and Reebok Instructor News, Volume 5, Number 2, 1997

recipes

breakfasts

If you think skipping breakfast is an easy way to cut some calories, think again. Miss out on this essential meal and your blood-sugar levels will be up and down all day. The result? You'll eat more, and it's likely to be junk food at that. So get your fill with these daybreak delights.

Skinnier cooked breakfast *sal*

What could be better at the weekend than to treat yourself to a cooked brekkie without the guilt – you just need to think grill not frying pan and poached not fried. Breakfast has always been a big part of my life. When I was growing up, my parents went out to work on the farm early each morning, returning at 9.30 to a cooked breakfast that set them up for the day, which is, after all, what breakfast should be all about.

serves 2
prep time 5 minutes
cooking time 15 minutes
472 calories per serving

2 good-quality pork sausages
2 large field mushrooms, peeled if necessary and stalks trimmed
sea salt and freshly ground black pepper
1 teaspoon sunflower oil
2 large free-range eggs
2 large tomatoes, halved
4 slices of Parma ham
toasted soda bread, to serve

tip

For perfect poached eggs, buy the freshest, best-quality (organic if possible) ones you can. Drop into boiling water and reduce the heat immediately so that the water is barely moving and the eggs cook gently.

Preheat the grill until hot.
Fill a large, deep frying pan with boiling water and bring to the boil.
Cut the skin off the sausages, remove the sausage meat and form into four patties. Season the mushrooms, brush with the oil and place on the grill pan with the sausage patties. Cook near the top of the grill for 4 minutes. Turn the sausages and mushrooms and grill for a further 3 to 4 minutes.
Meanwhile, carefully crack the eggs into the boiling water and reduce the heat so that the water barely moves. Poach the eggs for 4 to 5 minutes until the whites are set, but the yolks are still soft.
While the eggs are cooking, return to the grill and remove the sausages and mushrooms and keep warm. Season the tomatoes, place on the grill pan and grill for 2 minutes on each side.
Meanwhile, heat a non-stick frying pan until hot.
Remove the eggs one at a time with a fish slice and drain any excess liquid on to a piece of kitchen towel before placing one on each plate.
Dry-fry the Parma ham slices in the hot frying pan for 1 minute each side and divide between the plates along with the sausage patties, mushrooms and tomatoes. Serve immediately with the toasted soda bread.

Fantastic coconut and mango oatmeal *sophie*

Porridge really is a good way to start the day, especially with our English winters, and this recipe gives porridge a new lease of life. No longer do I want to hear it called gruel! I have replaced normal milk with coconut milk and added mango and toffee-like muscovado. Squeeze over an aromatic lime – you'll love it.

serves 2
prep time 10 minutes
cooking time 12 minutes
318 calories per serving

90g old-fashioned, large oats
200ml tin reduced-fat or light coconut milk
salt
1 medium to large mango
1 teaspoon dark muscovado sugar
1 lime, cut into 8 wedges

Place the oats, coconut milk and a pinch of salt in a non-stick saucepan with 225ml cold water. Bring to the boil and simmer for 10 minutes, stirring occasionally to prevent sticking.
While keeping an eye on the saucepan, peel and cube the mango.
When the oat mixture is cooked through, serve topped with the mango cubes, a sprinkling of sugar and a couple of wedges of lime per person on the side.

tip

Swap the coconut milk for skimmed milk to save 66 calories.

Asparagus eggs Benedict *gizzi*

This is the perfect brunch dish (though it works well as a light lunch or supper too). Replacing smoked salmon or ham with asparagus and the hollandaise sauce with Parmesan make this eggs Benedict much healthier than its traditional cousin.

serves 2
prep time 5 minutes
cooking time 10 minutes
246 calories per serving

1 wholemeal muffin
a bunch of asparagus (about 14 stalks), ends trimmed
2 free-range eggs
20g shaved Parmesan
olive oil
salt and freshly ground black pepper

Split the muffin in two and pop in the toaster until toasted and golden. Bring two pans of salted water to the boil.
Throw the asparagus into a pan and boil for 2 to 3 minutes until tender, but still holding some 'bite'. Drain and set aside somewhere warm.
Carefully break an egg into the other pan, reduce the heat to a low simmer and poach gently for 2 to 5 minutes until the white sets around the yolk.
Repeat with the other egg. The more confident you get with poaching, the more likely you'll be able to poach two eggs at a time. Remove the eggs from the pan with a slotted spoon and drain on kitchen paper.
To serve, lay one half of the muffin on each plate. Top with half the asparagus, one egg and half the Parmesan. Finally, drizzle with a little oil and sprinkle on some salt and pepper. Cut into the runny egg yolk to make a delicious, oozy sauce.

tip
Try turning it into something extra special by using duck eggs and a little truffle oil.

Stewed rhubarb with toasted pistachios *happy*

Rhubarb is one of the great joys in food. Its flavour is entirely its own and the colour of it is a pure miracle. Just having a jar of something so vibrant and pretty in the fridge door is enough to make you happy. This is a real favourite to have on standby for that moment when you can't quite put your finger on what you fancy.

serves 2
prep time 5 minutes
cooking time 15 minutes
156 calories per serving

250g rhubarb, roughly chopped
1cm knob of ginger, peeled and finely grated
2–3 tablespoons orange blossom honey (or other clear honey)
20g shelled pistachios, roughly chopped

Wash the rhubarb thoroughly in a colander under the tap and place straight into a heavy-based saucepan without shaking off too much of the excess water. Add the ginger, place a lid on top, and turn the heat to medium. Give the pan a gentle stir after 5 minutes to make sure that the rhubarb isn't catching on the bottom, replace the lid and carry on cooking for about another 10 minutes.
Meanwhile, toast the pistachios in a dry frying pan. When they start to turn golden and smell nutty, set them aside on a plate.
Once the rhubarb is cooked, add the honey and leave to cool. Store in a jar in the fridge until needed. Serve either cold or warm, topped with the green pistachios.

tip
This is great either on its own or served over yoghurt for breakfast. This is also brilliant as the base for a quick crumble or a soufflé if you're feeling cheffy.

Sweetcorn fritters with avocado and bacon *gizzi*

Don't be freaked out by the avocado, lean bacon and maple syrup combo, it works really well.
If you're still not convinced, simply leave out the syrup (you'll save on the calories too).

serves 2
prep time 10 minutes
cooking time 10 minutes
394 calories per serving

for the fritters
1 large free-range egg
150g 0% fat Greek yoghurt
1 tablespoon cornflour
60g polenta flour (or plain flour is fine)
salt and freshly ground black pepper
200g tin sweetcorn, well drained
2 spring onions, thinly sliced
olive oil spray
for the topping
4 slices of smoked bacon medallions or back bacon, all fat cut off
    to leave just the eye meat (the round piece)
½ avocado, sliced
1 tablespoon maple syrup

In a bowl, mix together the egg, yoghurt, cornflour, polenta flour and
salt and pepper until it becomes a smooth batter. Add the corn and spring
onion and mix thoroughly.
Heat a non-stick frying pan until it's fairly hot and spritz with some oil.
Spoon in half of the fritter mixture and cook for 1 to 3 minutes or until the
bottom has turned crisp and golden. Using a wide spatula or fish slice, flip
over carefully to cook the other side for 1 to 2 minutes. Repeat with the rest
of the mixture to make a second fritter.
Meanwhile, heat a griddle pan, spritz with the oil spray and griddle all four
pieces of bacon for 1 to 2 minutes on each side.
Serve each fritter with two slices of bacon and a few slices of fanned out
avocado. Drizzle with half the maple syrup to serve.

tip
With all the toppings,
this recipe is a fantastic
weekend treat. Lose the
toppings and save 124
calories per serving.

Boursin, pancetta and chive omelette *sophie*

This makes a lovely brunch dish at the weekend. I dry-fry the pancetta and use low-fat Boursin, so even though it seems very naughty, it really isn't too bad. When a dish is as simple as this, always try and buy the best ingredients, and that means organic eggs if you can.

serves 1–2
prep time 5 minutes
cooking time 12 minutes
269 calories per serving
without cheese save an extra 70 calories

3 large free-range eggs, beaten
50ml semi-skimmed milk
2 tablespoons finely snipped chives
salt and freshly ground black pepper
3 slices of pancetta
100g Boursin Light or any other low-fat garlic cream cheese, chilled

Preheat the grill to very hot.
Take a medium bowl and whisk the eggs, milk, chives and some salt and pepper together.
Cut the pancetta into little strips and dry-fry in a frying pan over a medium heat for around 5 minutes.
Add the egg mixture and then crumble in the cheese. Stir around the edges of the pan and then let settle and cook for 2 minutes. Finally pop under the grill for 4 minutes or until set.

Huevos rancheros *gizzi*

A classic Mexican breakfast traditionally served with refried beans. I've ditched them to make a lighter breakfast, but if you wanted to make more of a meal of it, then they would be the perfect accompaniment.

serves 2
prep time 5 minutes
cooking time 10 minutes
317 calories per serving

for the tomato sauce
1 small onion, finely chopped
2 cloves of garlic, peeled and finely chopped
olive oil spray
1 hot red chilli
230g tin chopped tomatoes
salt and freshly ground black pepper
4 small corn tortillas or 2 large flour tortillas
4 free-range eggs

Gently fry the onion and garlic in a spritz of olive oil for 5 minutes or until they have softened but not browned. Add the chilli and fry for a minute, then add the tomatoes and simmer for about 5 minutes until slightly reduced – you want a pourable sauce. Season to taste.

Meanwhile, bring a pan of salted water to the boil. Carefully break an egg into the other pan, reduce the heat to a low simmer and poach gently for 2 to 3 minutes until the white sets around the yolk. Repeat with the other eggs. The more confident you get with poaching, the more likely you'll be able to poach a few eggs at a time. Remove the eggs from the pan with a slotted spoon and drain on kitchen paper.

Heat the tortillas up by placing them on a hot dry frying pan for a few seconds on each side.

To serve, split the tortillas between two plates, topping them with the eggs and a generous spoonful of sauce.

tip

Adding a tablespoon of white wine vinegar to the water before adding the eggs will stop the eggs breaking up during poaching.

Tangerine, passion fruit, mango and coconut smoothie *hangy*

Okay, here it is … the hangover cure. This smoothie is the most incredible custard-yellow drink to make everything all right again – a balm to soothe liver and soul. When you're feeling fragile, this is SO much better than a greasy fry-up.

serves 2
prep time 3 minutes
146 calories per serving

4 tangerines or small oranges, cut into halves
200ml tin reduced-fat or light coconut milk
1 ripe passion fruit, halved and scraped out
1 small ripe mango

tip
Try this with ice or more tangerine juice if you fancy something slightly lighter.

Squeeze the oranges into the bowl of a blender (with one hand cupped to filter any pips). Add the coconut milk and passion fruit.
Cut the cheeks off the mango and put the flesh in with the rest of the fruit before whizzing it up.

'Smoothies are the perfect fast food – they only take seconds to whizz up.'

Pink smoothie *heavy*

This is an excellent little booster to have mid-morning (try taking it to work in an empty jar, giving it a shake before drinking) or when you feel that your energy levels have dipped. Also brilliant for breakfast, it only takes seconds to make and is really rather filling … not to mention fabulous to look at.

serves 2
prep time 3 minutes
97 calories per serving

4 juicing oranges, quartered
1 pomegranate, quartered
1 banana

Using your hands (I don´t believe in all the new-fangled gadgets out there at all), squeeze the oranges and pomegranate into the bowl of a blender, catching the pips and unwanted pith as you go. Add the banana and blend until smooth. If you find this mixture slightly too thick, simply add a little water or the juice of another orange.

It's key with any smoothie to use a blender that liquidizes its contents and doesn't just chop it all up. This wants to end up like liquid pink silk.

Sunshine smoothie *sal*

This is perfect to make quickly and drink on the run if you think you have no time for breakfast. Other fruit to try in your smoothies are pineapple, strawberries, raspberries, blueberries and nectarines. You can also experiment with different juices such as apple, pomegranate and grapefruit.

serves 2
prep time 5 minutes
156 calories per serving

1 large frozen banana (see the tip below)
1 medium mango (350–400g), roughly chopped
1 ripe peach, stoned and roughly chopped
225ml freshly squeezed orange juice

To freeze bananas, peel, wrap in clingfilm and freeze overnight. Perfect for smoothies or to eat straight from the freezer like an ice cream.

Remove the banana from the freezer 20 minutes before you need it. Using a handheld blender, whiz up the banana, mango, peach and orange juice for approximately 20 seconds until smooth.
Pour into two glasses and drink immediately.

Blueberry, raspberry, strawberry and orange juice *happy*

There is nothing like the colour of bright fruit first thing in the morning to fill you with energy and make you happy. Maybe it's because, to me, it's like eating the sun that fed the fruit themselves. In addition to which, all the fruit in this juice are very high in vitamin C and antioxidant properties, which will really boost your energy levels. This recipe is ready in minutes, isn't too sweet and is a joyful little number to have up your sleeve for when you want a lift.

serves 2
prep time 5 minutes
64 calories per serving

a handful of raspberries
a handful of blueberries
100g strawberries
juice of 4 small juicing oranges

To make it easy on yourself, or if you're always running late like me, make up little freezer bags with the right amount of red fruit and blitz from frozen with the orange juice. Also, make sure you freeze the fruit fast after buying or picking it to avoid squandering any of the precious, fresh vitamins (the longer you leave bought or cut fruit, the more vitamins you lose).

Pop all the ingredients into a blender **and whiz up until smooth.**

light
lunches

Gone are the days of limp lettuce leaves and cheap French dressing. The humble salad has come a long way, and guess what? Today's versions actually satisfy. Here are our favourite recipes for salads and other light lunches, guaranteed to impress your palate and your friends.

Sesame-crusted halloumi salad

When eating vegetarian food, the textures, colours and flavours must all come together like a symphony. This salad has the crunchiness of the lettuce and cucumber, which works well with the softness and nuttiness of the cheese, while the coldness of the salad is good with the warmth of the dressing. To make it non-vegetarian, just add some cooked chicken strips.

serves 4
prep time 10 minutes
cooking time 5 minutes
210 calories per serving

for the salad
120g romaine lettuce, ripped into bite-sized pieces.
2 large spring onions, thinly sliced
¼ cucumber, peeled and cut into quarters
½ punnet of salad cress
12 Pomodorino or cherry tomatoes, halved
200g light halloumi cheese, drained and cut into 8 slices
25g sesame seeds
1 teaspoon olive oil
for the dressing
4 tablespoons mango chutney
1 teaspoon white wine vinegar
12 drops of Tabasco
salt and freshly ground black pepper

Divide the lettuce, spring onion, cucumber, salad cress and tomatoes between two plates.
Dip the halloumi slices into the sesame seeds to completely coat.
Heat a large frying pan over a medium heat, add the oil and fry the halloumi for 2 to 3 minutes, turning once and pressing them down a little with a fish slice until golden and slightly melted.
Remove and top each salad with the cheese.
Off the heat, quickly add the mango chutney, white wine vinegar and Tabasco to the frying pan with 80ml water. Bubble for 20 to 30 seconds and season well (be careful if tasting because it will be very hot). You may need a little more vinegar depending on which brand of mango chutney you use.
Pour the dressing over the salad and eat immediately.

tip
If you find that the sesame seeds don't stick to the halloumi very well, brush with a little egg yolk mixed with water.

Seared scallop, fennel and tarragon salad *sophie*

Scallops are a true delicacy and are quite costly, but for a special lunch they are fantastic. Fennel is also really good with any seafood, so if you haven't tried this combo before, it's a must. This is a good dish for a light lunch or starter.

serves 2
prep time 10 minutes
cooking time 10 minutes
435 calories per serving

200ml fresh orange juice
50ml Pernod or pastis
1 tablespoon olive oil
1 bulb of fennel, finely sliced
1 red onion, finely sliced
a handful of tarragon
salt and freshly ground black pepper
6 diver-caught scallops, cleaned

Firstly, make the dressing by putting the orange juice and Pernod in a saucepan. Cook for around 7 minutes until only a third of the liquid is left and it has a syrupy-ish consistency, then whisk in the olive oil. Dress the fennel and red onion with half of the dressing, add the tarragon leaves and season.
Heat up a frying pan until very hot. Season, then sear the scallops for about 1 minute on each side. You really want to get a lovely golden look without overcooking.
To serve, pile up the salad and top with the scallops, then drizzle with the rest of the dressing.

Tuna and flageolet salad

This recipe originated with my friend Antonia while on a skiing holiday when we were just fondued and tartifletted out by all the cheese and meats. This is a great storecupboard salad (apart from the salad leaves) and it was all available in an Alpine supermarché! If you don't have any romaine lettuce or rocket, they could be swapped for some little gem or curly leaf lettuce and the radishes could be substituted with tinned sweetcorn.

serves 2
prep time 10 minutes
cooking time 10 minutes
260 calories per serving

2 large free-range eggs
2 tablespoons extra-virgin olive oil
2–3 teaspoons aged balsamic vinegar, plus extra for serving
½ small clove of garlic, peeled and crushed
¼ teaspoon Dijon mustard
salt and freshly ground black pepper
200g tinned flageolet beans, rinsed and drained
1 stick of celery, sliced
¼ head of romaine lettuce, ripped into bite-sized pieces
20g rocket
75g radishes, trimmed and sliced
80–100g drained tuna in spring water

It is important to use a good balsamic vinegar, aged for at least 10 years. If you don't have this at hand, simmer the balsamic vinegar until more syrupy and allow to cool before using. Also, it's worth trying to get hold of the best eggs, preferably organic, that you can for this recipe.

Place the eggs in a saucepan of boiling water, bring back to the boil and simmer for 7 minutes for softly boiled eggs. Remove immediately and cool under cold running water. Shell and cut into halves.
Meanwhile, whisk together the olive oil, balsamic vinegar, garlic and mustard with ½ tablespoon water and season well. Alternatively, shaking in a jam jar ensures the dressing emulsifies together properly.
Toss the dressing through the flageolet beans, celery, lettuce, rocket and radishes.
Divide the salad between two plates. Top with the tuna and halved eggs and serve immediately with a little more balsamic vinegar drizzled over the top.

Watercress, pear and goat's cheese salad with honey-glazed pecan nuts *honey*

This salad rocks. The flavours of pepper in the leaves, sweet pear, nutty pecan and sour goat's cheese are a terrific combination. Ideal as a light lunch or supper, this recipe is a great way to remind ourselves that salad IS fun. Goodbye iceberg and Hello watercress.

serves 2
prep time 10 minutes
cooking time 10 minutes
215 calories per serving

20g pecan nuts
½ teaspoon set sunflower honey
  (or whatever honey you like works as well)
a little salt
20g strong, hard goat's cheese, thinly shaved
50g watercress
1 firm pear, such as Conference or Flamingo, cored
  and thinly sliced lengthways
for the dressing
1 teaspoon Dijon mustard
2 teaspoons sherry vinegar
3 teaspoons olive oil
½ teaspoon clear honey

tip

In order to achieve really crunchy pecans, it is key to separate them on the plate while you're cooling them down and to wait until they're completely cold. Also, look for pears that are slightly on the hard side of life, as a bit of bite is a brilliant way of introducing texture in salads generally.

Toast the pecan nuts in a hot non-stick frying pan for 5 minutes, keeping them on the move to avoid catching. Once well toasted, add the set honey to the pan to coat the nuts in the sizzling hot liquid and sprinkle with a little salt. Set aside and leave to cool thoroughly on a plate.
Combine the dressing ingredients with the help of a sauce whisk or put them into a jar and give it a shake.
In a big bowl, mix together the pear, the watercress and the goat's cheese shavings with the cooled pecan nuts. Dress the salad and serve immediately.

Peppered mackerel and watercress dip with pitta crisps

Everyone loves a dip and it is easy to eat a whole calorie-laden pot with crisps or tortilla chips. This dip uses the oiliness of the fish to give you the taste factor and the savouriness of the baked pitta crisps to cut through it. Great as a snack for sharing or to serve as a starter in little dishes.

serves 6
prep time 5 minutes
cooking time 10 minutes
257 calories per serving

4 wholemeal pittas
200g skinned, peppered smoked mackerel fillets
30g watercress, large stalks removed
1 teaspoon English mustard
100g light cream cheese
70g low-fat natural yoghurt
a good grating of whole nutmeg
1½ tablespoons lemon juice
salt
watercress, to garnish

Preheat the oven to 200°C/fan 180°C.
Split each pitta into two and cut each half into dipping-sized triangles then place them on a baking tray. Bake in the oven for 8 to 10 minutes until crisp, then remove and keep warm.
Meanwhile, put the mackerel, watercress, mustard, cream cheese, yoghurt, nutmeg and lemon juice into a food processor and whiz until everything is combined. Season with salt and serve the dip garnished with the watercress and alongside the pitta crisps. You can keep this in the fridge, covered, for up to 2 or 3 days.

tip

This also works well with smoked salmon and a little horseradish sauce instead of the mustard. To make spicy pitta crisps, brush the pittas with a little olive oil and sprinkle with paprika before cutting up and baking.

90 light lunches

Sundried tomato and black olive dip *sophie*

With all the flavours of Italy in a bowl, this fresh dip is an antidote to those high-fat dips that you get in the shops. Of course you can miss out the anchovies if you want, but they don't overpower the dip, they just add more punch.

serves 6 as a snack or pre-dinner nibble
prep time 5 minutes
90 calories per serving

50g sundried tomatoes
50g black olives, pitted
1 teaspoon capers, drained
4 tomatoes, roughly chopped
2–4 anchovy fillets, drained
1 tablespoon finely chopped basil
2 tablespoons white wine vinegar
1 clove of garlic, peeled
2 tablespoons extra-virgin olive oil
freshly ground black pepper

Pop all the ingredients in a blender and blitz. Check the seasoning, but it probably won't need much salt due to the capers and anchovies.

'I love serving this with breadsticks and some freshly cut crudités.'

Chicken Caesar salad
with Melba toasts *gizzi*

I often find Caesar salad dressings too rich. This extremely low-fat version is so much lighter, but is still packed full of flavour. It would be just as delicious with griddled king prawns.

serves 2
prep time 10 minutes
cooking time 20 minutes
372 calories per serving (with anchovies)

2 boneless free-range chicken
  breasts, skin off for extra
  skinniness
olive oil spray
salt and freshly ground
  black pepper
2 slices of soya and linseed bread
3 little gem lettuces
6 fresh anchovy fillets (optional)

for the dressing
1 small clove of garlic, peeled and grated
2 anchovy fillets in olive oil from
  a jar
salt and ground white pepper
3 tablespoons 0% fat Greek yoghurt
a squeeze of lemon juice
20g freshly grated Parmesan
  (with a microplane)

Heat a griddle until smoking. Spritz the chicken breasts with a little oil and season with salt and pepper. Place onto the griddle and turn down the heat. Cook for 5 minutes, turn over and repeat for 5 more minutes, or until cooked through. Remove from the heat and leave to rest for 5 minutes, then cut into 7mm slices widthways.

Preheat the oven to 200°C/fan 180°C. To make the Melba toasts, toast the soy and linseed bread until golden. Cut off the crusts and slice through the bread horizontally so that you are left with two sides of bread, each with one toasted side and one soft side. Place on a baking tray, soft-side-up, and bake for 5 minutes or until the bread has curled up and dried.

Place the garlic, anchovy and some salt and pepper in a pestle and mortar and pound until broken into a smooth paste. Tablespoon by tablespoon, add the yoghurt and lemon juice until combined. Stir in the Parmesan and season again to taste.

Drop the lettuce leaves into a bowl and mix together with the dressing. Place on a plate and top with the chicken breast and fresh anchovies. Lay the Melba toasts by the side.

Thai duck and watermelon salad *gizzi*

This salad also works very well with guinea fowl or quail for a fancy change. Serve this dish as a starter, a light lunch or before my Thai green curry (page 123) for an easy dinner party.

serves 2
prep time 10 minutes
cooking time 10 minutes
373 calories per serving

½ small watermelon
   (about 400g), peeled,
   seeded and chopped
   into 2–2.5cm cubes
2 tablespoons coriander leaves
2 tablespoons mint leaves
1 tablespoon sunflower seeds
1 x 300g (or 2 x 150g) duck
   breasts, skin off
olive oil spray
salt and ground white pepper
2 shallots, thinly sliced
2 teaspoons olive oil

for the dressing
2 spring onions, finely sliced
1cm knob of ginger, peeled and finely
   shredded
1–1½ small red chillies, chopped
1 tablespoon very finely shredded
   lemongrass stalk (outer layer removed)
1 tablespoon lime juice
1 tablespoon fish sauce
1 teaspoon brown sugar

In a bowl, mix together the watermelon, coriander, mint and sunflower seeds.

Heat a griddle until smoking. Spray the duck breast with oil and season with the salt and white pepper. Lay on the griddle and cook for 2 to 3 minutes on each side depending on the size. This should give you perfect medium-cooked duck. Remove from the heat and leave to rest for 5 minutes.

In a pestle and mortar, grind together the dressing ingredients and the juices from the duck. Pour over the salad, mix together and leave to infuse for 5 minutes.

Meanwhile, fry the shallots in the olive oil for 2 to 3 minutes or until they are crisp and golden. Drain on kitchen paper.

Slice the duck into 7mm slices and toss through the salad. Serve the salad immediately topped with a sprinkling of the crispy shallots.

tip

There are lots of types of chillies available these days and the general rule is the smaller the chilli, the hotter it is. I like using small bird's eye chillies in this dish.

Pepperoni and Parmesan pitta pizzas _sal_

In the time it takes to ring your order through to the local pizza takeaway and for it to be delivered, you could have cooked the pizza, eaten it and tidied up, saving probably half the calories and half the money.

makes 4
prep time 10 minutes
cooking time 10 minutes
287 calories per pizza

4 white pitta breads
400g tin chopped tomatoes with herbs
2 pinches of caster sugar
2 pinches of hot chilli powder
2 sundried tomatoes, thinly sliced
4 thin slices of pepperoni, shredded into strips
1/4 small red onion, thinly sliced
1/2 small yellow pepper, thinly sliced
8 green olives, pitted and halved
5g freshly grated Parmesan
30g ricotta cheese
a small handful of shredded basil leaves
a handful of wild rocket leaves
balsamic vinegar

Preheat the oven to 220°C/fan 200°C.
Run a sharp knife 1cm in from the edge of each pitta bread and follow the outline to remove the top layer of bread and create a border for the pizzas. Place the pittas directly onto the top shelf of the oven and cook for 2 minutes to crisp up.
Meanwhile, place the chopped tomatoes in a sieve to remove all the excess juice. Divide the tomatoes among the pittas and spread out evenly. Sprinkle each with the sugar and chilli powder. Top with the sundried tomatoes, pepperoni, red onion, pepper and olives. Sprinkle over the Parmesan and dot the ricotta on top.
Bake the pittas directly on the oven shelf for 8 minutes or until cooked. Serve immediately, scattered with the basil and rocket leaves and drizzled with balsamic vinegar.

tip

Alternative toppings could include canned tuna, sweetcorn, courgette, Parma ham or spring onions. You could also use olive oil instead of balsamic vinegar to season the pizzas once cooked and wholemeal instead of white pitta breads.

Chargrilled mint and yoghurt lamb on a beetroot and feta salad

sophie

My parents live in Greece so I spend a lot of time there. The food is brilliant and this is a light lunch inspired by our lovely summertime meals under the grapevine. The colours are beautiful together and it tastes pretty good too. The Greek diet is hailed as one of the healthiest in the world (it's down to all the lovely olive oil) so tuck in with pleasure.

serves 2
prep time 10 minutes
cooking time 10 minutes (plus 10 minutes resting time)
482 calories per serving

½ teaspoon ground cumin
½ teaspoon ground coriander
½ teaspoon ground cinnamon
salt and freshly ground black pepper
2 lean lamb leg steaks
40g rocket
1 lemon

for the beetroot and feta salad
150g packet of cooked beetroot, peeled
a bunch of spring onions, thinly sliced
75g feta cheese, well drained
25g pine nuts
salt and freshly ground black pepper
1–2 tablespoons olive oil

for the mint and yoghurt dressing
100g 0% fat Greek yoghurt
a small handful of mint
1 clove of garlic, peeled
salt and freshly ground black pepper

Mix all the spices together with some salt in a bowl and rub into the lamb. Heat up a griddle pan.

While this is happening, quarter the beetroot and mix together in a bowl with the spring onion. Crumble in the feta. Lightly toast the pine nuts and add to the bowl. Finally, season and sprinkle with a little olive oil, then mix thoroughly.

When the griddle pan is smoking, you can start cooking the lamb. The steaks need about 4 minutes each side and then need to rest for 10 minutes. I like them served pink.

With a handheld blender, blitz together the yoghurt, mint and garlic, then season and blitz again until smooth. In a separate bowl, dress the rocket with the meat juices and a squeeze of lemon.

I serve this on a big platter. Start with a layer of rocket, then beetroot salad then the slices of lamb. Finish off by drizzling over the yogurt dressing.

lunch on the go

Sometimes life is so busy we barely have time to grab a pre-packed sandwich from the corner shop. Food on offer in train stations, airports, even the high street can be pretty awful – high in calories and fat, low on quality. It only takes a little bit of planning with these tempting but easy ideas.

Egg and cress sandwich on rye bread *handy*

Egg and cress is a killer combo and this recipe is full of flavour. Cress sadly disappeared off the radar for a little while, which is a huge shame since it's one of the few things that we eat that's pretty much growing up until the point where it hits our palates. Here's to the classic ones never dying out.

makes 2
prep time 5 minutes
cooking time 10 minutes
242 calories per serving

2 medium free-range eggs
1 teaspoon low-fat natural yoghurt
1 teaspoon Dijon mustard
1 teaspoon mayonnaise
1 punnet of mustard cress
salt and white pepper
4 thin slices of rye bread

Cook your eggs into a pan of boiling water for 8 minutes before running them under cold water (they like the 'eggcercise'… Sorry!) until cool. In a small bowl, mix together the yoghurt, the mustard and mayonnaise. With a pair of scissors, chop the cress into the bowl before adding the cooled eggs. Mash up the mixture with a fork before seasoning well and making up the sandwiches.

Please don't compromise on the quality of the eggs that you use. It is really important to make sure that you buy eggs from happy, free-range, preferably organic, chickens. This simple recipe is great because the filling can be made the night before and will keep for a couple of days in the fridge. You could even chop up half a spring onion and add it to the mix if you fancied a change.

Bresaola, fennel and horseradish on toasted rye bread *harvey*

This sandwich is a punchy little number. It is the antidote to wet, petrol-station sandwiches; it is shouting from the rooftops, not simpering under a blanket. This is such a great recipe for taking to work, on picnics, or even serving as a canapé (simply cut into quarters, omit the top layer of toast and replace with a shaving of Parmesan or Pecorino).

serves 2
prep time 5 minutes
180 calories per serving

4 teaspoons creamed horseradish sauce
4 thin slices of rye bread, toasted
8 slices of good-quality bresaola
1 small bulb of fennel, super-thinly sliced
a squeeze of lemon juice

Unless you are good with vegetables and a sharp knife, here is an occasion to wheel out that favourite friend: the mandolin. It is important to use super-thin slices of fennel here otherwise the poor beef is in danger of being 'fenneled'.

Spread the horseradish onto the slices of bread and top with the bresaola and fennel. Season with a tiny squeeze of lemon juice and off you go.

'Strong condiments like horseradish are a great way to add flavour without loading up on calories.'

Tuna niçoise wrap *gizzi*

Salade niçoise is such a popular salad and by putting it in a wrap and making it portable, you can enjoy it on the go. This sandwich, with its lean proteins and a colourful selection of vegetables all bundled up in a flour tortilla, really is the perfect packed lunch.

serves 2
prep time 5 minutes
cooking time 10 minutes
305 calories per serving

1 free-range egg
8 green beans
2 large flour tortillas
1 tablespoon low-fat mayo
4 little gem lettuce leaves
185g tin tuna in spring water
2 small vine tomatoes, quartered
2 teaspoons capers in white wine vinegar
2–3 purple olives, pitted and halved

Hard-boil the egg for 7 minutes and quarter. Blanch the green beans in boiling salted water for 3 minutes and rinse under cold water to refresh. For each wrap, lay out a flour tortilla and spread the middle with half the mayonnaise. Lay on two lettuce leaves, two quarters of egg, half the can of tuna, four beans, one tomato, 1 teaspoon capers and 2 or 3 olive halves. Fold the bottom of the tortilla up and the top down and then fold the sides in to form a neat package. Cut diagonally in half and serve.

tip

If you're taking this to work, wrap it, before cutting, in clingfilm and cut in half when you come to eat it.

'Gone are the days of a salad
only ever featuring combinations
of lettuce, tomato and cucumber.'

Smoked trout and beetroot salad

This salad offers everything that you look for when eating food – not only colour and texture, but also tastes that explode in your mouth. This is a quick throw-together dish that is ideal for an impromptu starter to any dinner party or for a lunch, whether at home or packed up.

serves 2
prep time 15 minutes
214 calories per serving

40g rocket
40g baby spinach leaves
2 x 80g smoked rainbow trout fillets, flaked
20g pumpkin seeds
120g cooked baby beetroot, each cut into 6 wedges
1 tablespoon capers, rinsed and drained
2 tablespoons virtually fat-free fromage frais
½ teaspoon horseradish sauce
zest of ¼ lemon
½–1 tablespoon lemon juice
salt and freshly ground black pepper

Divide the rocket, baby spinach leaves, smoked trout, pumpkin seeds, beetroot and capers between two plates.
Mix the fromage frais, horseradish sauce, zest and lemon juice with 1 tablespoon water and season well.
Drizzle the dressing over the salad and serve immediately.

Add some orange zest and juice instead of lemon for a variation.

Lentil salad with Mediterranean vegetables and goat's cheese *gizzi*

This is good as a light lunch you can impress your friends with, but also makes a delicious packed lunch. Lentils are great at lunchtime because they really fill you up, meaning you're more likely to avoid mid-afternoon snacking.

serves 2
prep time 5 minutes
cooking time 20 minutes
531 calories per serving (with goat's cheese)
371 calories per serving (without goat's cheese)

240g mixed Mediterranean vegetables, such as tomatoes, peppers, artichoke hearts, courgettes and aubergines, roughly chopped
2 teaspoons olive oil
2 teaspoons balsamic vinegar
sea salt and freshly ground black pepper
200g green lentils (preferably Puy lentils), rinsed and well drained
300ml chicken or vegetable stock
a handful of basil leaves, torn
100g chèvre goat's cheese, sliced horizontally into two discs

Preheat the oven to 200°C/fan 180°C.
Put the Mediterranean vegetables in a small roasting tray and toss with half the olive oil and vinegar and a sprinkle of the sea salt.
Roast for around 15 minutes or until the vegetables just begin to soften, but still retain their shape (some may be ready before others).
Meanwhile, place the lentils in a pan and cover with the stock, then bring to the boil. Boil for 20 minutes or until the lentils have absorbed all the liquid and are tender. Cover with a lid.
Place the lentils in a mixing bowl along with the roasted vegetables, remaining balsamic vinegar and olive oil, seasoning and basil and mix thoroughly (putting the vegetables into the hot lentils enables them to absorb all the flavours). Leave to cool.
Heat the grill on high. Place the two halves of the goat's cheese onto some foil and grill for 1 to 2 minutes or until bubbling and golden (alternatively you can use a blow torch if you have one). For a portable lunch, place the salad in a medium-sized Tupperware container and top with a round of goat's cheese.

'Who would have thought that you could make lentils so sexy?'

soups

Shop-bought soups can be deceptively calorific, packed with unnecessary fat and even sugar. And diet soups? Don't even go there, unless musty-tasting water is your thing. Making your own is 'souper' simple. Skip the cream and croutons and choose a hunk of wholegrain bread, some rye crackers or oatcakes on the side to fill you up further.

Tomato, chilli and basil soup

sophie

This is my favourite instant soup. There is no excuse for buying ready-made soups when this one takes hardly any prep time and just needs to be simmered for half an hour. It also doesn't have any of the nasties that are in some ready-made soups – no flour, chemicals or additives. And when tomatoes are cooked it brings out an antioxidant called lycopene, so you even get more benefits than you would from eating them raw.

serves 4
preparation time 15 minutes
cooking time 40 minutes
95 calories per serving

1 tablespoon olive oil
1 onion, finely chopped
2 cloves of garlic, peeled and crushed
a pinch of dried chilli flakes (more if you like it HOT)
400g tin plum tomatoes
salt and freshly ground black pepper
a small pinch of sugar
a handful of roughly chopped basil
2 tablespoons low-fat crème fraîche

Heat up the oil in a saucepan and gently sweat the onion and garlic until translucent. Add the chilli and cook for another minute.
Add the tomatoes and then fill the empty tin with water, twice, and add them to the pan.
Season with the salt, pepper and sugar. Bring the soup to the boil and then reduce to a simmer for 30 minutes.
Add the basil to the soup and spoon in the crème fraiche. Finally, blitz until smooth with a handheld blender. Check the seasoning and serve. The soup will keep for up to 3 days in the fridge.

tip
To make this soup a bit lower in calories, you could leave out the crème fraîche.

Virgin Bloody Mary soup

Everyone's idea of a perfect Bloody Mary is different, so put the Tabasco, celery salt and Worcestershire sauce on the table so your guests can season to their taste. For the 'hair of the dog' version, drizzle a little vodka over before serving.

serves 4
prep time 10 minutes (plus 30 minutes melting time)
55 calories per serving

700g very ripe tomatoes on the vine
3 large sticks of celery
½ medium red onion
350ml tomato juice
½ teaspoon Worcestershire sauce
15 drops of Tabasco
½ teaspoon celery salt
a pinch of sugar
2 teaspoons sherry vinegar
6 ice cubes
finely chopped celery and chives, to serve

Cut a cross in the bottom of each tomato and place in a bowl. Pour over boiling water and leave for 20 to 30 seconds. Remove and cool under cold running water. Peel the skins from the tomatoes, cut into quarters and remove the seeds.
String the celery by snapping each end of the celery stick and pulling along the length of each one to remove any stringy bits. Alternatively, use a potato peeler.
Whiz the tomatoes, celery, onion, tomato juice, Worcestershire sauce, Tabasco, celery salt, sugar and sherry vinegar in a food processor until quite smooth.
Pour into a jug with the ice cubes and allow to melt, which will take about 30 minutes.
Serve the soup in bowls topped with the finely chopped celery and chives.

As an alternative, serve this soup in tumblers with a celery stalk as a stirrer.

Smoked aubergine soup with harissa and orange *harry*

The texture of this soup is so silky that it's hard to believe that there isn't even a teaspoon of oil in the entire soup. The flavours have a strong Tunisian feel and are as deep as the layers of sand in the Sahara desert.

serves 2
prep time 5 minutes
cooking time 15 minutes
102 calories per serving (with topping)
without topping save 20 calories

1 small aubergine
¼ teaspoon rose harissa
375ml really good hot chicken stock
100g tinned chickpeas, drained
juice of 1 orange
salt and freshly ground black pepper
for the topping (optional)
2 teaspoons Greek yoghurt
finely grated zest of ½ orange

Place the aubergine directly onto a large flame, such as that from a barbecue or a gas ring, and with the help of a pair of tongs, turn it occasionally so that the vegetable ends up being slightly charred all over. If you don't have a gas hob, use the grill and keep turning the aubergine to achieve a similar result. This process takes roughly 10 minutes and is the making of this soup.

When the aubergine is all smoky and has surrendered some of its shape, peel it with your fingers and place into the bowl of a blender along with all the other ingredients. Whiz until smooth, then warm the soup up if necessary, season well and serve with a teaspoon of Greek yoghurt and a little orange zest.

tip
Smoking the aubergine in this way creates the most intense flavour and is responsible for most of the taste in this recipe.

Mushroom and chestnut soup *handy*

This soup not only has the most wonderful flavour but is naturally rich and silky from the chestnuts. It is superbly versatile and perfect for a picnic lunch in a Thermos, taken in a jar and heated up for lunch at the office or as a starter. Timeless and elegant, it's hard to believe that you can whiz this recipe up in less than half an hour.

serves 2
prep time 10 minutes
cooking time 25 minutes
209 calories per serving (without garnish)

½ tablespoon olive oil
75g shiitake mushrooms, roughly chopped
125g chestnut mushrooms, roughly chopped
125g portabellini mushrooms, roughly chopped
1 small onion, roughly chopped
100g ready-roasted chestnuts
500ml good-quality chicken stock (or vegetable or game stock)
salt and white pepper
luxury tip: garnish
2 slices of serrano ham or prosciutto
a few drops of truffle oil

tip

I have chosen a mixture of different mushrooms here, but you could use whatever was in season or available. The flavour of white and button mushrooms, however, is just too insipid and would not stand up to the chestnut. This recipe would be unbelievably delicious with wild mushrooms such as girolles or chanterelle that already have a ton of flavour if you're feeling flush.

Preheat the oven to 250°C/fan 230°C.
In a very large saucepan, fry the mushrooms in the olive oil for 10 minutes over a high heat till golden all over. Add the onion and chestnuts and turn down the heat. Stir for a couple of minutes to avoid burning any of the ingredients, then pour in the stock and bring to the boil. Simmer for another 10 minutes before whizzing in the blender until smooth. Season well with salt and the white pepper.
For the garnish, pop the ham in the oven for a couple of minutes until crispy. Top the soup with a slice of crispy ham, a few drops of the truffle oil.

'Replace a handful of meals per week with our delicious soups and you'll be well on your way to dropping a dress size.'

Chicken and mushroom risotto soup *gizzi*

This is a rustic, earthy soup that really fills you up. Play around with the ingredients, perhaps changing the chestnut mushrooms to mixed wild mushrooms when in season or shredding up a smoked chicken for added flavour. It's also a great recipe to make with leftover roast chicken. You can keep any leftover soup in the fridge for a few days or freeze it.

serves 6
prep time 5 minutes
cooking time 35 minutes
332 calories per serving

2 teaspoons olive oil
1 onion, finely chopped
3 cloves of garlic, peeled and chopped
300g risotto rice
200ml dry white wine
2 litres chicken stock
200g chestnut mushrooms, wiped and sliced
1 tablespoon low-fat crème fraîche
1 tablespoon flat-leaf parsley, finely chopped
20g freshly and finely grated Parmesan
1 cooked free-range chicken breast, skinned and shredded
salt and freshly ground black pepper

Heat half the oil in a pan and gently fry the onion and garlic over a low heat for 5 minutes until softened. Add the rice and fry for a further minute, stirring and coating the rice with the oil.
Pour in the wine and stir until it has all been absorbed. Pour over the chicken stock and bring to the boil. Reduce to a simmer and cook for 15 minutes or until the rice is tender (the soup actually benefits from the rice being a little more cooked than for a normal risotto). The soup will be fairly thin, but will fill out once all the other ingredients have been added.
Meanwhile, heat a large frying pan and fry the mushrooms in the remaining teaspoon of olive oil for 5 minutes or until golden brown.
Once the risotto is cooked, stir through the crème fraîche, parsley, Parmesan, chicken and mushrooms. Season to taste.

tip
For a skinnier version take out the Parmesan

Hot-and-spicy chicken soup *sal*

This is a very light broth that packs a punch with the Eastern flavours of the lemongrass, ginger and coriander. If you like it spicy, add more chilli or just leave the seeds in.

serves 2
prep time 10 minutes
cooking time 25 minutes
178 calories per serving

750ml chicken stock
1/4–1/2 red chilli, deseeded and very finely chopped
1 small lemongrass stalk, outer leaves removed and finely chopped
1 teaspoon tamarind paste
1/2 teaspoon grated fresh ginger
a handful of coriander, stalks left whole and tied in a little bundle
    and leaves roughly chopped
160–180g skinless free-range chicken breast
1 spring onion, finely sliced
2 tablespoons fish sauce
1 1/2–2 tablespoons lime juice

Bring the stock to the boil in a saucepan with the chilli, lemongrass, tamarind paste, ginger and stalks of the coriander.
Once boiling, gently lower the chicken breast into the stock and simmer for 20 minutes, covered. Turn the chicken over halfway through the cooking time.
Discard the coriander stalks and remove the chicken breast. Thinly slice the chicken and add back into the soup with the spring onion, chopped coriander, fish sauce and lime juice.
Reheat the soup and when piping hot, serve.

tip
The chicken stock needs to be natural in colour, which the chilled ones often are. Generally, the more expensive the stock (try organic brands), the better quality it will be.

Proper chicken soup *sophie*

Whenever I feel ill, down, homesick or hungover, this is what I crave. I will actually get off my sickbed and go out and buy the ingredients, it's that good. People think it's an old wives' tale that chicken soup is good for curing flu, but there is an enzyme that comes out of the chicken in the cooking process that really does help. Chicken soup also happens to be very filling and low in calories, so you can have quite a few bowls without feeling guilty!

serves 6
prep time 10 minutes
cooking time about 3 hours
165 calories per serving

1 parsnip, cut into quarters
2 carrots, cut in half
1 leek, trimmed and cut in big pieces
2 sticks of celery, cut into big pieces
1 onion, cut into big pieces
1.8–2kg free-range chicken
2 bay leaves
a handful of flat-leaf parsley
salt and freshly ground black pepper

Put the parsnip, carrot, leek, celery and onion into your biggest saucepan with the chicken. Cover with 3 litres cold water and add the bay leaves and half the parsley, stalks and all.
Slowly bring to the boil and then turn right down. Leave just below a simmer and cook for 3 hours.
Strain the stock into another saucepan (thus removing all the vegetables and meat).
Slice the carrots and add back to the stock and, finally, add some chopped chicken back in (I usually add the two breasts back into the soup and make the rest into a Thai chicken salad or use for sandwiches).
Sprinkle over a handful of chopped parsley and check the seasoning.
Et voilà! You can keep this soup in the fridge for up to 3 days or freeze any extra.

tip
To turn this into a more filling meal, add some pasta or noodles to the strained stock and cook for a further 15 minutes, then finish with a drizzle of truffle oil.

No-fuss split pea and ham soup *gizzi*

By using a ham stock cube, you make this normally fussy soup totally fuss-free. It truly is wonderful because it's warming and will keep you full for hours.

serves 6 (refrigerate any leftover soup for a few days or freeze)
prep time 15 minutes (plus overnight soaking)
cooking time 55 minutes
268 calories

olive oil
1 onion, chopped
1 carrot, chopped
1 leek, white part only, trimmed and chopped
1 stick of celery, chopped
2 cloves of garlic, peeled and chopped (optional)
300g yellow split peas, soaked overnight, then rinsed and well drained
1.5 litres ham stock (chicken stock is fine if you can't find it)
2 bay leaves
200g thick, sliced ham from the deli counter, shredded
1 tablespoon curly parsley, finely chopped
salt and freshly ground black pepper

Heat a splash of olive oil in a large pan. Add the onion, carrot, leek, celery and garlic and sauté over a very low heat for 10 to 12 minutes or until they have softened and begun to go golden.

Add the split peas, give a good stir, then cover with the ham stock and add the bay leaves. Bring up to the boil, then slow down to a simmer. Cook for 30 to 40 minutes or until the peas are tender. Remove and discard the bay leaves.

Pour bit by bit into a blender and purée until smooth. Put the soup back into the pan with the shredded ham and parsley and warm through. Season with salt and pepper and pour into bowls.

tip
Try to chop all the vegetables into similar-sized pieces because this will help them to cook evenly.
For a veggie alternative leave out the ham and replace the ham stock with vegetable stock. At 213 calories,¡ it's a winner.

main meals

All your favourites, from comfort-food classics to sin-free fast food. Each of these dishes has been lovingly created with maximum taste and satisfaction in mind. There is nothing on these pages we wouldn't choose ourselves in preference to the full-fat originals. Try them and you'll be converted, too.

Risotto with prawn, lemon, spring onion and basil *sophie*

Risottos are usually rich and packed full of butter and cheese, but this version is very light and much lower in fat. Risottos are versatile and you can use whatever flavour combo you want, but seafood works especially well in this lighter recipe because Italians never add cheese to fish or seafood risottos (or pasta either).

serves 2
prep time 5 minutes
cooking time 20 minutes
471 calories per serving

olive oil
½ onion, finely chopped
1 clove of garlic, peeled and finely chopped
150g risotto rice
75ml white wine
750ml warm light vegetable stock
a bunch of spring onions, thinly sliced
150g cooked peeled prawns
3 tablespoons low-fat crème fraîche
a squeeze of lemon
½ bunch of basil, chopped
salt and freshly ground black pepper

Heat up a splash of oil and gently fry the onion and garlic until translucent. Add the rice and continue frying for 2 minutes. Add the wine and continue stirring until the wine is absorbed. Now start to add the stock, ladle by ladle, stirring until the stock is absorbed between each spoonful. Give the risotto lots of tender loving care by stirring regularly and the creamy starch will come out of each grain. Continue like this for 10 to 15 minutes. Add the spring onion to the risotto, continue cooking for 5 minutes and then add the prawns and crème fraîche.

Now, this is the important point. You need the rice to be al dente, which means firm to bite (not soft and overcooked) so keep tasting it until it is time to take it off the heat (it will probably need another 5 minutes). Add a squeeze of lemon and stir through the basil. Check the seasoning and then, for the final touch, grate some lemon zest over the top.

tip

There are so many possible variations. Try crab or chicken instead of the prawns or replace the basil with chives or tarragon.

Easy Thai green prawn curry with fragrant rice *gizzi*

It's good to take advantage of the amazing authentic ingredients available at the supermarkets these days and if you're lucky enough to live by an Asian supermarket, go and see what fantastic gems they have there. The rice is a wonderful accompaniment to this aromatic Thai curry and is worth the time, but if you don't want the fuss, simple basmati rice works just fine.

serves 2
prep time 10 minutes
cooking time 20 minutes
542 calories per serving

400ml tin reduced-fat or light
  coconut milk
1 heaped tablespoon Thai green
  curry paste
2 tablespoons fish sauce
1 teaspoon light brown sugar
juice of ½ lime
2 lime leaves, finely sliced or 1
  teaspoon lime leaves from a jar
200g raw peeled king prawns
50g peas
50g fine beans, cut in half

50g sugar snap peas, cut diagonally
  in half
50g asparagus tips
a small handful of coriander
for the fragrant rice
100g basmati rice
salt
1 lemongrass stalk, smashed and cut
  in half
1 red chilli, deseeded and cut in half
3 slices of ginger
1 clove of garlic

Place the rice, salt, lemongrass, chilli, ginger and garlic in a saucepan. Cover with enough water to come 1cm over the top of the rice. Bring to the boil and simmer for 8 minutes, covered. The rice should have absorbed almost all of the water, but still be a bit wet. Remove from the heat and leave, covered, to absorb the remaining water for 10 minutes. Remove the lemongrass and chilli before serving.

Meanwhile, heat the coconut milk in a saucepan. Add the curry paste and stir until dissolved. Stir in the fish sauce, brown sugar, lime juice and lime leaves, then add the prawns, peas, beans, sugar snap peas and asparagus tips. Poach for 3 minutes or until the prawns are pink and firm and the vegetables are cooked but are still holding some crunch. Do not boil otherwise it may curdle. Top the curry with a sprinkling of coriander and serve with the rice.

tip

Try and use an authentic fish sauce if you can, such as Squid brand nam pla. For the Thai green curry paste, I use Mae Ploy.

Spice-crusted salmon *sal*

I read in a newspaper clipping in one of my granny's old cookbooks that 'salmon is a luxury, but one does occasionally indulge in luxuries'. It is time to make salmon luxurious once more. This is a bizarre combination of flavours that works, with the sweetness and savouriness of the sugar and thyme complementing the fruity fieriness of the salsa. Everything can be done ahead of time (the salsa tastes even better if you can leave it for an hour) and you can then just last-minute cook the salmon. The salmon and salsa are even delicious the next day served in a flour tortilla as a wrap.

serves 2
prep time 20 minutes (plus 10 minutes marinating time)
cooking time 12 minutes
325 calories per serving

1 large clove of garlic, peeled
1 tablespoon unrefined light muscovado sugar
1/4–1/2 teaspoon dried chilli flakes
2 teaspoons fresh thyme leaves
1 teaspoon fennel seeds
1 tablespoon lime juice
2 x 150g salmon fillets, skin on
1/2 teaspoon sunflower oil
salt and freshly ground black pepper

Preheat the oven to 200°C/fan 180°C.
While the oven is heating up, make the mango salsa (see page 189) and leave it in the fridge.
Use a pestle and mortar to make a paste from the garlic, sugar, chilli flakes, thyme, fennel seeds and lime juice.
Place the salmon fillets, skin-side-down, on a non-stick baking tray, brush the salmon flesh with the oil and season well.
Spoon the paste over the flesh of the salmon and marinate for 10 minutes.
Bake the salmon in the oven for 11 to 12 minutes, depending on the thickness of the fillets, or until just cooked through (don't overcook it).
Leaving behind the skin on the baking tray (the flesh should easily come away), serve the salmon with mango salsa.

If you can stand the smoke, fry the salmon fillet, flesh-side-down, in about a teaspoon of oil in a hot frying pan for 45 seconds and then bake in the 200°C oven for 8 minutes for a barbecued effect.

Fish and chips with mushy peas

Once in a while you can't beat walking along the seafront eating fish and chips out of the paper. But how do you get the flavour of chip-shop fish and chips without all the fat? Believe me, this has been a challenge, and in the end some butter did have to be added to crisp up the topping for the fish. So here goes with my attempt at a lower-fat version of a dish that is a national treasure.

serves 4
prep time 20 minutes
cooking time 45 minutes
403 calories per serving

for the chips
1 teaspoon sunflower oil
1 free-range egg white
1/4 teaspoon freshly ground black pepper
1/4 teaspoon salt
1/4–1/2 teaspoon mild chilli powder
400g potatoes, such as King Edwards,
    unpeeled and cut into 1cm wide chips

for the fish
75g slightly stale white bread
a handful of flat-leaf parsley
2 tablespoons chopped chives
1 tablespoon capers, rinsed and drained
zest of 1 lemon
20g butter, melted
1 tablespoon plain flour
1 large free-range egg, beaten
salt and freshly ground black pepper
4 x 175g plaice fillets, trimmed
lemon wedges, to serve

for the mushy peas
250g frozen peas
2 tablespoons 0% fat Greek yoghurt
a small handful of chopped mint leaves
zest of 1/2 lemon
1 1/2 tablespoons lemon juice
salt and freshly ground black pepper

Preheat the oven to 200°C/fan 180°C.

For the chips, rub the oil over a non-stick baking tray. Whisk the egg white with the black pepper, salt and chilli powder until frothy. Toss the potatoes in the egg white and pour onto the baking tray. Separate the chips out and cook in the oven for 45 minutes, turning every 10 minutes. Don't be alarmed by how they look in the early stages of cooking; the chips will crisp up, so persevere.

Meanwhile, to make the topping for the fish, whiz together the bread, herbs, capers and lemon zest in a food processor until rough breadcrumbs form, then stir through the melted butter.

Place the flour, beaten egg and breadcrumb mixture on separate plates. Season the flour well and then dunk each plaice fillet, flesh-side-only, in the flour, followed by the egg and then the breadcrumbs.

Place the fish onto a large non-stick baking tray and bake on the top shelf of the oven 12 minutes before the chips are done. Don't overcook the fish. The thinner the fillet, the less time it will take to cook.

While the fish and chips are cooking, cover the peas with water, bring to the boil and boil for 4 minutes.

Drain and mash the peas with the yoghurt, mint, lemon zest and juice and season well.

Serve the fish and chips together with the mushy peas and a wedge of lemon.

tip

Other types of fish that can be used are trout fillets, mackerel fillets, haddock and cod. For a crispier topping to the fish, after cooking in the oven, place under a medium grill (not too near the top) and grill until crispier. The chips also work really well by substituting the salt, pepper and chilli powder with 1 to 1½ teaspoons Cajun spice and continuing as above.

'Your average chip-shop cod and chips is 950 calories, so we're saving you over 500 calories and I promise you won't be disappointed.'

Thai seafood and vermicelli noodle salad *sophie*

I first had this dish on a beach in Asia with a rather dishy Italian boyfriend of mine. Suffice to say that the surroundings were beautiful and it was a little chunk of paradise. And when it came to food, we had a habit of ordering extra chilli and lime with everything (to the point of it being our catchphrase). Funnily enough, the cutie has gone, but they are still two of my most-loved ingredients and this dish is a firm favourite.

serves 2
prep time 10 minutes (plus 1 hour chilling time)
cooking time 5 minutes
363 calories per serving

100g thin rice noodles
a bunch of spring onions, thinly sliced
5cm knob of ginger, peeled and chopped
1 chilli, deseeded and finely chopped
a small handful of chopped coriander
a small handful of chopped mint
150g mixed cooked seafood (if you have a fishmonger, you can
    choose your favourite combination, if not, most supermarkets
    sell ready-mixed packs)
100g cooked peeled king prawns
juice of 3 limes
2 tablespoons rice vinegar
1 tablespoon fish sauce
1 tablespoon sweet chilli sauce
½ iceberg lettuce, to serve in (also works well with radicchio)

Firstly, fill the kettle up and bring to the boil. Put the noodles in a bowl and cover with the boiling water. Leave to soak for 5 to 6 minutes, stirring halfway through to separate. Drain the noodles and refresh in cold water, then drain again very well.
Mix together the spring onion, ginger, chilli and herbs. Mix in with the noodles and then add all of the other ingredients except for the lettuce. Chill for 1 hour and then serve the salad in the iceberg lettuce leaves.

Healthy roast dinner *sophie*

This is my comfort food. Roast chicken hits all the spots when I'm feeling down and makes a fabulous meal in winter with braised red cabbage and in the summer with a salad. This chicken is healthier because I've bulked out the potatoes with squash, while cooking the potatoes in their skins means they absorb less fat and keep all their nutrients. With lots of immune-system boosting garlic and fragrant rosemary, it is packed full of flavour.

serves 6
prep time 20 minutes
cooking time 1 hour 15 minutes
338 calories per serving

1 lemon
a couple of sprigs of rosemary, chopped
a couple of sprigs of thyme, chopped
6–8 cloves of garlic
sea salt and freshly ground black pepper
olive oil
1.8–2kg free-range chicken
300g new potatoes
½ butternut squash, peeled and chopped into medium-sized pieces
2 red onions, quartered
250ml white wine

Preheat the oven to 220°C/fan 200°C.
Finely grate the zest from the lemon and mix in a bowl with the herbs, 2 cloves of the garlic, peeled and chopped, and some salt and pepper. Add a teaspoon of olive oil and rub the mixture between the skin and the chicken breast. Now this isn't a glamorous job, but it does make it taste good. You basically pull the skin up off the breast, keeping it attached. You then stick your fingers up between the skin and meat and rub the mixture in. Finally, halve the lemon and pop inside the chicken cavity.
Put the chicken in a roasting tray and cook for 20 minutes, then turn the temperature down to 190°C/fan 170°C and continue roasting for another 50 minutes. I sometimes turn the chicken to cook breast-side-down halfway through cooking because this keeps it very moist, though it is less visually appealing because the skin doesn't crisp so much.
Place the potatoes, squash, red onion and remaining garlic cloves in a separate roasting tray and sprinkle with a little olive oil and sea salt.

The vegetables need to go in for the last hour.

When the time is up, put the chicken and vegetables onto a plate, cover and leave to rest for 10 minutes.

Put the tray onto the heat and add the wine. Season and let bubble away for a couple of minutes, stirring and making sure that you get all the chicken residue from the bottom of the pan.

Serve the roast (chicken skin off) with French beans or broccoli stir-fried with chilli and garlic.

Crispy chicken with home-made coleslaw *happy*

This recipe was thought up for one of the girls on *Cook Yourself Thin*, who was addicted to takeaway deep-fried chicken. Not only is it super-quick to make, but by altering the cut of chicken or the coleslaw ingredients, you can tailor it to what you fancy. So if you're an addict too, it'll feel like you're choosing from a takeaway menu. It's best to have a mandolin to slice the vegetables. Apart from being one of the most wonderful words in the English language, a mandolin is key when 'thinly' slicing anything. It's a super-cheap piece of equipment and has transformed my relationship with raw vegetables – you'll never look back.

serves 2
prep time 20 minutes
cooking time 15 minutes
290 calories per serving

1 large free-range chicken breast
1 free-range egg white
40g fine polenta meal
15g freshly and finely grated Parmesan
a good pinch of cayenne pepper
½ tablespoon olive oil
½ lemon, cut into wedges
salt and freshly ground black pepper
for the home-made coleslaw
4 small radishes, top and tailed
½ small red onion
½ small bulb of fennel, top and tailed
50g red cabbage
35g celeriac, peeled
75g Greek yoghurt
1 teaspoon sherry vinegar
salt and freshly ground black pepper

This coleslaw recipe is a really nifty way of hitting one of your 'five a day' without really trying. Also, you could use any number of other vegetables such as carrot, celery, white cabbage, white onion and even apple, depending on what you like and what's in season. This is one of my favourite combinations of vegetables, maybe because it ends up looking bright pink! If you are after a white version of this recipe, substitute the red cabbage and red onion for white ones.

Cut the chicken breast into super thin strips of roughly the same size. Lightly whisk the egg white in a medium-sized bowl. In another bowl, combine the polenta, Parmesan and cayenne pepper.
Dip each chicken strip first in the egg white and then in the polenta mixture until well covered. Set aside on a large plate. When all the chicken strips are coated, heat the oil in a non-stick frying pan. Cook the chicken for 7 minutes each side, over a medium high heat, until it is cooked through and the outside is crispy and golden. Season to taste.
While the chicken is cooking, use a mandolin (I like using the 'julienne' setting for the celeriac) to thinly slice all the vegetables into a big bowl. If you don't have a mandolin, you can cut it by hand with a sharp knife, but it will take around 10 minutes. Once all the vegetables are cut into thin slices, pour in the yoghurt and the vinegar and toss thoroughly.
Season well and serve with the crispy chicken, a sprinkling of cayenne and some lemon wedges for those who fancy a bit of an edge.

Lebanese chicken kebabs with garlic sauce and pickles *gizzi*

A kebab is notoriously naughty – packed full of creamy sauces, fatty meat and normally served with chips. Not this one. It's made from lean chicken in a light marinade and it's served with a Lebanese twist by adding mixed pickles and garlic sauce for a superb flavour.

serves 2
prep time 10 minutes (plus 12–24 hours marinating time)
cooking time 10 minutes
365 calories per serving

for the marinade
2 cloves of garlic, peeled
    and chopped
1 tablespoon olive oil
a pinch of smoked paprika
salt and white pepper
2 free-range chicken breasts,
    cut into 2cm strips

for the garlic sauce
150g 0% fat Greek yoghurt
1 clove of garlic, peeled and grated
1 tablespoon chopped flat-leaf parsley
a squeeze of lemon juice
salt

for the wrap
2 large flour tortillas
4 leaves of little gem lettuce
2 small vine tomatoes, quartered
6 cornichons
6 jalapeño pepper slices
a dash of Tabasco

To make the marinade, stir together the garlic, oil, paprika and seasoning. Add the chicken and mix thoroughly. Cover and refrigerate for at least 12 hours.
To make the garlic sauce, mix together the yoghurt, garlic, parsley, lemon juice and a pinch of salt. This can be made up to a day in advance if it's easier for you.
Heat a griddle pan until smoking. Thread the pieces of chicken on to two wooden skewers (if you soak the skewers before using them, they will not burn). Lay the kebabs on to the griddle and cook for 5 minutes on each side or until cooked through.
Lay the wraps on two plates and spread over the garlic sauce. Lay two lettuce leaves on each, one of the tomatoes, three of each of the pickles and finally top with a kebab and a dash of Tabasco. Fold the base up towards the middle and the sides in. Serve immediately.

Chicken tikka masala
with fragrant rice *gizzi*

What is generally considered to be the most popular of curries is also one of the most calorific, but by simply removing the ghee (clarified butter) and swapping the cream for coconut milk, we get a lighter, tastier version. This dish requires a little forethought because you need to marinate the meat, but is worth it for the result.

serves 2
prep time 10 minutes (plus 12–24 hours marinating time)
cooking time 45 minutes
526 calories per serving

for the marinade
1 tablespoon tikka masala
   curry paste
150g 0% fat Greek yoghurt
2 free-range chicken breasts,
   each cut into 5–6 large chunks
salt

for the sauce
1 rounded tablespoon tikka masala curry paste
1 onion, finely chopped
200g passatta
200ml tin reduced-fat or light coconut milk
1 tablespoon 0% fat Greek yoghurt
a handful of coriander, chopped

for the fragrant rice
100g basmati rice
salt
5 curry leaves
1/2 teaspoon black mustard seeds
1 cinnamon stick
a pinch of saffron (optional)

To make the marinade, mix the curry paste, yoghurt, chicken and salt together, cover and leave overnight in the fridge to absorb all the delicious flavours.

Preheat the oven to 220°C/fan 200°C. Wipe the marinade off the chicken and place, piece by piece, onto a baking tray. Bake for 10 minutes or until slightly charred, but not cooked through. You are just trying to get some colour here because the chicken will finish cooking in the curry sauce. Set the tikka chicken aside while you make the sauce.

Heat the curry paste in a saucepan. Add the onion and sweat slowly over a low heat for 5 to 8 minutes or until the onion is translucent and soft. It is important to take the time to do this slowly because the onion will then

release its natural sugars, producing a sweeter dish, but be careful not to do this over too high a heat because the curry paste will burn. Add the passatta and coconut milk and bring to the boil. Turn down the heat and add the tikka chicken. Cook over a low heat for 5 minutes or until the chicken is cooked through. Finish by stirring through the yoghurt and coriander.

To make the fragrant rice, add the rice, a pinch of salt and the aromatics to a pan and cover with enough water to come 1cm over the top of the rice. Bring to the boil and simmer for 8 minutes, covered. The rice should have absorbed almost all of the water, but still be a bit wet. Remove from the heat and leave to absorb the remaining water for 10 minutes, covered. Remove the cinnamon stick before serving with the curry.

'The ready-meal version can be up to a whopping 840 calories. Add half a naan, an onion bhajee and a couple of beers and you're pushing 1500 calories . . . for one meal!'

Mexican burgers *sophie*

I love Mexican flavours, although this is more Tex-Mex, I suppose. I also adore avocados. They are full of good fats and add a beautiful, buttery texture to dishes – a great replacement for mayonnaise. The colours and flavours of this dish are brilliant and it's great for a summer barbecue.

serves 4
prep time 20 minutes
cooking time 10 minutes
456 calories per serving

for the burgers
400g turkey mince (must be the best quality or even try and
    get a butcher to mince it for you)
1 shallot or small onion, finely chopped
1 clove of garlic, peeled and very finely chopped
1 teaspoon ground cumin
1 teaspoon ground coriander
½ teaspoon smoked paprika
a pinch of dried chilli flakes
for the guacamole
1 avocado
1 clove of garlic, peeled
1 lime
salt and freshly ground black pepper
for the salsa
4 ripe tomatoes, chopped
½ red onion, chopped
120g tinned blackeye beans
a splash of olive oil
juice of ½ lime
a handful of coriander
½–1 chilli (depending on how hot you like your food), finely chopped

4 flour tortillas
½ iceberg lettuce, shredded
150g 0% fat Greek yoghurt
1 lime, cut into wedges
jalapeño peppers

Mix all the burger ingredients together and make into eight patties. Set aside.

To make the guacamole, scoop out all the avocado flesh and put into a blender with the garlic and lime juice. Blend until smooth and season to taste.

To make the salsa, mix the tomato and onion with the beans, olive oil, lime juice, coriander and chilli. Season and set aside.

Heat up a griddle pan. Cook the burgers for about 5 minutes on each side, turning occasionally to chargrill all over.

Heat up a frying pan (with no oil) and warm the tortillas through. If using granary rolls, cut them in half. Serve the burgers with some shredded lettuce, a dollop of yoghurt, the guacamole and salsa, wrapped in a tortilla or squashed in a roll. Serve the lime and the jalapeño peppers on the side for extra flavour and heat.

Jalapeño peppers are great because they add lots of flavour and no fat.

'Hot and spicy food is like a party for your palate, and when you truly savour a taste, you eat less overall.'

Chicken and prawn egg-fried rice

Stir-frying is an art form and often people overcook the meat, undercook the vegetables and add oil rather than water if the food sticks to the wok. Stir-frying, as its name suggests, is stirring and frying and that is what you need to continually do with this method of cooking. It's so quick that all the ingredients must to be prepared before you even start to cook. If you take the time to do that, you will have a perfect stir-fry every time.

serves 4
prep time 15 minutes
cooking time 20 minutes
402 calories per serving

200g pure basmati rice, rinsed
2 tablespoons sweet chilli sauce
2 tablespoons light soy sauce
1 tablespoon toasted sesame oil
1½ tablespoons sesame seeds
1 tablespoon sunflower oil
1 free-range chicken breast,
   cut into 2cm cubes
130g raw peeled king prawns

50g mangetout, cut in half
½ red pepper, sliced
3 spring onions, sliced
1 large clove of garlic, peeled and
   crushed
20g knob of fresh ginger, peeled
   and grated
2 large free-range eggs, beaten
2 handfuls of roughly chopped coriander

Bring a large saucepan of water to the boil, add the basmati rice, stir once, and bring back to the boil. When the rice comes to the boil, it will appear to be 'dancing in the water' and this is when the timer should be started and the rice boiled for 8 minutes or until al dente. Place the rice in a sieve, cover with a sheet of kitchen towel and allow to stand for 5 minutes to absorb any excess water.

Meanwhile, mix the sweet chilli sauce together with the soy sauce and the toasted sesame oil and set aside.

Heat a wok over a high heat until nearly smoking. Add the sesame seeds and stir-fry for 30 seconds until browned, then remove.

Add the oil and swirl around the wok to heat through. Stir-fry the chicken for 1 minute before adding the prawns and cooking for another 1½ minutes. Remove and place in another sieve for any excess oil to drain away.

To the wok, add the mangetout and red pepper with 2 tablespoons water and stir-fry for 1½ minutes with a lid on if you have one.

Add the basmati rice, spring onion, garlic and ginger and stir-fry for a further 2 minutes.

Move the rice to the side of the wok and pour the egg onto the base of the wok. The egg should be in quite large pieces, so resist the temptation to mix it in too soon. Leave for 30 seconds to set a little before stirring through the rice with the chicken, prawns, two-thirds of the coriander, the sauce and the sesame seeds.

Toss to mix everything thoroughly and serve immediately. Sprinkle with the remaining coriander.

tip

It is worth spending the money on pure basmati rice because often there are fewer broken grains in the pack, which means less starch in the water when you cook the rice and so the grains are less likely to stick together. If you then soak the rice for at least 20 minutes before cooking, the cooking time is reduced by about 2 minutes and the rice will be even more light and fluffy.

Steak and kidney pie *harry*

This recipe is light, aromatic and utterly wonderful. I promise that it won't clobber you over the head with the flavour of the kidneys, so you will want to eat it all year round. This is what you might call a 'blonde' take on a masculine old classic.

serves 6
prep time 30 minutes
cooking time 2 hours 30 minutes
452 calories per serving

90g ready-rolled puff pastry (preferably a brand made with butter)
a little milk, to brush over the pastry
4 free-range lamb's kidneys, trimmed by the butcher
1 tablespoon buckwheat flour (you could use plain)
1kg good-quality lean free-range braising steak, cut into chunks
½ teaspoon white pepper
1 tablespoon olive oil
800g shallots, peeled and quartered
1 star anise
1 stick of cinnamon
1 bay leaf
150ml vermouth
700ml good-quality beef stock

Preheat the oven to 200°C/fan 180°C.
Roll out the sheet of puff pastry and divide into six triangles of roughly the same size (or cut out fun shapes of whatever you fancy – for the show we used a cow-shaped pastry cutter and some stars!). Brush the tops with a little milk and set onto a baking tray. Bake in oven for 15 minutes or until puffed up and golden. Set aside for later.
If you haven't already got the butcher to do this for you, slice the kidneys widthways with a sharp knife. With the help of little pair of scissors, carefully snip around the lighter centre core and discard. Then chop the livers into cubes.
In a large mixing bowl, combine the buckwheat flour, the steak, the kidneys and white pepper until evenly coated.

In a really large saucepan, fry half the meat in half the olive oil until it is well browned, then set aside. Repeat the process for the other half until all the meat is well coloured. Replace the meat into the pan, along with the shallots, star anise, cinnamon, the vermouth and stock. Bring to the boil, then turn the heat right down and place a lid over the top.

Simmer super-duper-gently for 2 hours before removing the lid and tasting. The meat may not need the last half an hour or it may want slightly more (it all depends on the steak that you are using, the size of the chunks and the pan). What you are looking for is meat that has surrendered most of its tension without shredding into a mess.

Season well and top with a crisp of golden puff pastry on the top of each serving.

tip

This recipe will stand or fall on the quality of the meat that you buy, and by meat, I include the stock. This is when the expertise (and the jolly face) of your local butcher is necessary to the success of the dish. Not only will your butcher choose the right braising steak for the cooking time, he will also trim the kidneys, which is a messy job. And don't try to save time by removing the stage involving browning the meat. In a slow-cooked dish, this is where the lion's share of the flavour is coming from, so do it in batches to avoid ending up with a Nothing and Kidney Pie.

Carbonara

Carbonara is a dish that everyone loves because it's so comforting, but it is loaded with fat, especially if cream is used. By adding some herbs and spices to great-quality eggs (organic if possible) you won't notice that it's lower in fat because it's just as tasty.

serves 2
prep time 15 minutes
cooking time 15 minutes
443 calories per serving

1 small onion, finely chopped
1 teaspoon of extra-virgin olive oil
45g Parma ham, visible fat removed and ripped into pieces
150g linguine
2 large free-range egg yolks
20g freshly grated Parmesan
1 tablespoon finely chopped chives
a small handful of roughly chopped flat-leaf parsley
5–6 drops of Tabasco
salt and freshly ground black pepper

tip

If an onion doesn't need to be browned but just cooked, then use water instead of oil and simmer until tender. If you're pregnant (or feeding a baby or elderly person), you might want to choose a different dish as there is a threat of salmonella with raw eggs.

Place the onion in a large, deep non-stick frying pan with 150ml water and bring to the boil. Lower the heat to medium, cover and cook for 5 minutes (see below). Remove the lid, turn up the heat and cook for 2 to 3 minutes or until the water has evaporated.

Add the olive oil and the Parma ham and cook for 3 to 4 minutes until browned, stirring frequently. Remove from heat and keep warm.

Meanwhile, cook the linguine according to the packet instructions, adding ½ a teaspoon of salt to the cooking water.

In a large bowl, mix the egg yolks, Parmesan, herbs and Tabasco.

Drain the pasta when cooked, reserving 3 to 4 tablespoons of the cooking water.

Mix together the pasta, egg yolks and Parmesan mixture with the reserved cooking liquid, the onion and Parma ham. Season well. Serve immediately with a green salad.

Lasagne *sophie*

Lasagne is a firm favourite with everyone. Unfortunately, with all that pasta, creamy sauce and fatty beef, it can be a huge meal. My version replaces some of the pasta and meat with vegetables and compared to an additive-filled, processed version, this is much better for the waistline. All the Italian purists that I know will be up in arms, but for me this is a great dish that leaves me feeling full of energy.

serves 6
prep time 15 minutes
cooking time 1 hour 20 minutes
347 calories per serving

1 teaspoon olive oil
1 onion, finely chopped
2 sticks of celery, finely chopped
1 carrot, finely chopped
4 cloves of garlic, peeled and finely chopped
400g lean beef mince (must be the best quality
    or even try and get a butcher to mince it for you)
salt and freshly ground black pepper
315ml red wine
400g tin plum tomatoes
1 tablespoon tomato purée
1 bay leaf
½ teaspoon dried oregano
2 courgettes, thinly sliced lengthways
1 jar of roasted red peppers in brine
4 sheets of lasagne
for the cheese sauce
500ml semi-skimmed milk
a good grating of whole nutmeg
salt and pepper
3 tablespoons cornflour
1 teaspoon English mustard
80g mature Cheddar cheese

Heat up a big saucepan and add the olive oil. Sweat the onion, celery, carrot and garlic for around 5 minutes over a medium heat.

Heat a frying pan up until very hot and cook the seasoned beef, without any oil, in batches, then add the beef to the saucepan. The point of cooking the beef in batches is to get a good colour on it because this adds more flavour.

When all the beef is in the saucepan, turn up the heat and add the wine. Cook until the wine has all been absorbed and then add the tinned tomatoes, tomato purée, bay leaf and oregano. Season and simmer for 30 minutes or until rich and tasty. Preheat the oven to 180°C/fan 160°C.

Heat a griddle pan. Season the courgettes and lightly chargrill or sear on each side, then leave on a plate until assembling time. Drain the peppers and also add to the plate.

Now, make the cheese sauce. Heat the milk up gently with a good grating of nutmeg, some salt and pepper. Mix the cornflour with 50ml of the milk and whisk back into the milk, continuing to cook for 2 to 3 minutes until thickened. Add the mustard and half the cheese. Check the seasoning and set aside.

Now for the fun part. Take a baking dish and start layering up the ingredients. Start with a layer of meat, then peppers, then meat, then courgettes, then meat, then pasta and finally cheese sauce. Top with the rest of the cheese and bake for 20–30 minutes or until bubbling.

tip

I have used mature Cheddar cheese here because this means you can use less and get more flavour, thus reducing the calories. I have also used cornflour instead of the usual flour and butter roux, which cuts out a lot of extra fat.

Pork paper with a garlic, anchovy and lemon dressing *harvey*

This recipe is a total winner and perfect for a summer lunch or light supper. Crammed full of flavour and seriously straightforward, it combines the best of simple and strong flavours. If you were feeling naughty, maybe add a glass of white wine and a bit of ciabatta to the picture.

serves 2
prep time 20 minutes
cooking time 10 minutes
255 calories per serving

250g free-range pork tenderloin
100g baby spinach leaves
for the dressing
4 anchovy fillets, drained of oil and finely chopped
1 clove of garlic, peeled and finely chopped
1 tablespoon olive oil
juice of ½ lemon
¼ teaspoon Dijon mustard
freshly ground black pepper

Heat a griddle pan on a high heat while you prepare the meat.
Cut the tenderloin into 1cm slices and place between two sheets of clingfilm, about four at a time, leaving a bit of space around each slice. With the help of a rolling pin, gently bash out the meat so that it flattens evenly until it is about as thick as a fat matchstick or as thin as you can manage without tearing it. Don't worry about being too exact; thin is good but this is food, not an exam.
With a pastry brush or your hands, wipe the surface of the meat with a little olive oil to prevent sticking and add the 'paper' pork to the hot pan. It is crucial that the meat doesn't overlap, so do it in batches if necessary. Leave the pork to sear well on one side (it will take roughly 4 minutes to get really good griddle marks depending on your pan), then flip briefly over for less than a minute.
While the pork is cooking, make your dressing by combining the anchovy and garlic with the olive oil, lemon juice, mustard and loads of black pepper.
Finally, pop a handful of spinach on the plates, top with three or four slices of pork and generously run the dressing over the lot.

tip
The flavours in the dressing are a moveable feast. If you don't like too much salt, cut back on the anchovy or rearrange the amount of garlic or lemon to suit your own taste.

Ho fan beef noodles *gizzi*

Not only is this recipe great because it cuts down on the fat by griddling, not frying, the meat, but you also get to regulate how you like your steak done by cooking it first. It's really important to use a good-quality oyster sauce because this is the base flavour – it's worth that trip down to Chinatown. Also, remember the secret to stir-frying is to have all your ingredients prepared before you start.

serves 2
prep time 10 minutes
cooking time 10 minutes
456 calories per serving

100g wide rice noodles
200g lean sirloin steak, trimmed of all fat
olive oil spray
salt and freshly ground black pepper
1 teaspoon olive oil
3 cloves of garlic, peeled and sliced
2cm knob of ginger, peeled and finely shredded
3 spring onions, cut in half widthways then lengthways through the middle
10 small shiitake mushrooms, 5 large ones cut in half
100g tenderstem broccoli, sliced lengthways through the middle
1 red pepper, deseeded and sliced
1 yellow pepper, deseeded and sliced
1 red chilli, sliced
for the sauce
3 tablespoons premium oyster sauce
2 tablespoons soy sauce

Boil the kettle. Place the rice noodles in a large bowl, pour over the boiled water and cover with clingfilm. Leave for 5 minutes or until tender. Drain and rinse under cold water to prevent them sticking together (they will heat up again when you add them to the stir-fry).
Heat a griddle pan until smoking. Spritz the steak with a little olive oil and season with salt and pepper. Place the steak onto the griddle pan and grill for 1 to 2 minutes on each side. This will give you a nice medium rare steak. If you like it more or less cooked, change the cooking time accordingly, but remember that when you add the steak to the stir-fry it will cook a little more. Remove from heat and leave to rest for 5 minutes. Slice thinly widthways.
To make the sauce, mix the ingredients together with a splash of water. Heat a wok. Add the olive oil and throw in the garlic, ginger, spring onion, shiitake mushrooms, broccoli and peppers and stir-fry for 2 minutes.
Pour over the sauce and add the noodles and steak. Give it a big stir until combined and serve topped with the chilli.

food for friends

How to be the perfect host:
1. wow your friends with moreish finger food and mouthwatering meals;
2. impress them with the fact your dishes are skillfully skinny;
3. spend minimal time in the kitchen because this food is so simple to prepare.

Fennel and lemon baked sea bass

Cooking for six people can seem daunting, but this dish allows you to relax. Cooked in a baking tray, this very impressive dish can be taken to the table for everyone to help themselves.

serves 6
prep time 15 minutes
cooking time 35–40 minutes
224 calories per serving

600g new potatoes
1 large bulb of fennel, trimmed, cored and thinly sliced
a handful of roughly chopped dill
12 green olives, pitted and roughly chopped
1 tablespoon extra-virgin olive oil
salt and freshly ground black pepper
1 large lemon, cut into 6 slices
6 sea bass fillets, skin on
100ml dry white wine
green salad, to serve

Preheat the oven to 200°C/fan 180°C.
Put the potatoes in a large pan of cold salted water and bring to the boil. Boil for 10 minutes before adding the fennel to the pan and cooking for a further 5 minutes.
Meanwhile mix the dill, olives and oil together.
Drain the potatoes and fennel and slice the potatoes into 1cm thick slices. Place the sliced potatoes and fennel on to a large baking tray and season well.
Evenly space out the lemon slices on top of the potatoes and fennel and cover each one with a sea bass fillet, flesh-side-up. Season well.
Top each sea bass fillet with a little of the dill and olive mixture.
Pour the wine in and around the potatoes with 4 tablespoons cold water and cover tightly with foil.
Cook on the top shelf of the oven for 20 to 25 minutes until the fish is just cooked.
Remove the foil and serve at the table, ensuring that everyone gets a fillet and a cooked lemon slice, which can be squeezed over the fish along with a little of the juice from the bottom of the tray. Serve with a green salad.

tip
If Jersey Royals are available, they are perfect for this dish. Otherwise use Vivaldi or Anya new potatoes. This recipe also works really well with mackerel or trout fillets.

Luxury fish pie *sophie*

Fish pie is super comforting, but it's one of those uber-rich, calorie-laden minefields. In this recipe I've topped the pie with tasty celeriac and made the sauce with white wine and low-fat crème fraîche. I've also added a little lobster for that touch of decadence.

serves 4
prep time 15 minutes
cooking time 1 hour 15 minutes
348 calories per serving (without optional lobster)

2 x 800g celeriac, peeled and cut into cubes
salt and freshly ground black pepper
2 leeks, trimmed and thinly sliced
2 cloves of garlic, peeled and finely chopped
2 tablespoons olive oil
100ml dry white wine
250ml fish or vegetable stock
1 heaped tablespoon cornflour
2 tablespoons low-fat crème fraîche
a handful of chopped flat-leaf parsley
200g salmon fillet, cut into 2.5cm cubes
1 raw lobster tail, peeled (optional)
220g mixed seafood (if you have a fishmonger, you can chose your favourite
    combination, if not, most supermarkets sell ready-mixed packs)

Put the celeriac into a saucepan, cover with water, bring to the boil and simmer for around 30 minutes or until tender. Drain well, season to taste and mash. Preheat the oven to 190°C/fan 170°C.

Sweat the leek and garlic in a deep frying pan with the olive oil for 4 to 5 minutes. Pour in the wine and stock and simmer for a couple of minutes. Mix the cornflour with 1 tablespoon water and stir into the leek sauce, then add the crème fraîche and parsley.

In a separate frying pan, fry the salmon, lobster and the mixed seafood if it's raw (if the seafood has already been cooked, just add it straight to the leek sauce) for about 2 minutes, just to get some colour.

Stir the salmon, lobster and seafood into the leek sauce. Check the seasoning and pour into a 25 x 20cm shallow baking dish.

Top with the celeriac mash and bake for 30 minutes or until golden brown.

tip

A ready-meal fish pie can contain well over 500 calories. For a good aphrodisiac boost, add some shelled oysters and their juices towards the end of cooking – yummy.

Poppy-seed tuna carpaccio with a wasabi and tangerine dressing *harry*

This recipe is blinking brilliant and the most fuss-free little stunner for a dinner party or summer lunch. All the flavours and colours here adore each other and are so clean and fresh that they will fill you with energy and buzz.

serves 6
prep time 15 minutes
cooking time 5 minutes
266 calories per serving

900g tuna loin (the best bit)
3 tablespoons poppy seeds
3 heads (200g) chicory, thinly sliced lengthways
150g radishes, sliced into matchsticks
1 punnet of shiso shoots or leaves (or sprouting beetroot or radish sprouts if unavailable)
1 punnet of fennel cress (or mustard, rocket or salad cress if unavailable)

for the dressing
1 teaspoon wasabi paste
4 teaspoons rice vinegar
2 teaspoons fish sauce
4 teaspoons vegetable oil
3 tablespoons freshly squeezed tangerine juice (use mandarin, clementine or orange if unavailable)

tip

If you wanted to make the dish slightly ahead of time, beware of dressing the carpaccio too long before serving. The acid contained in the vinegar, tangerine juice, wasabi and fish sauce will start to cook the fish as it stands. Wasabi is a strong flavour, so also make sure that you taste the dressing before serving to ensure that you're happy with it.

Heat a large non-stick frying pan until smoking.
Spread the poppy seeds out onto a plate. Press the tuna loin into the seeds so that they coat the surface of the fish on all sides except the ends. Place the fish into the hot pan and sear for a minute on all sides until there is a thin, pale, cooked band around the raw centre of the fish.
Transfer the tuna to a chopping board and slice as thinly as you can (roughly 5mm) without destroying the shape of the fish. Arrange onto a large plate and scatter with the chicory, radish, shiso and cress.
To make the dressing, simply mix all the ingredients together with a whisk and pour generously all over the dish. Let it stand for 5 minutes before serving to marry and marinate.

Saffron seafood linguine *harry*

This dish was concocted for one of the girls on *Cook Yourself Thin*, who loves big, colourful, flamboyant flavours but doesn't want to spend hours in the kitchen when cooking for dinner parties. This recipe is great fun and relies almost entirely on the quality of the ingredients, so if you are feeling frugal, don't bother!

serves 6
prep time 15 minutes
cooking time 20 minutes
530 calories per serving

600g raw whole king or tiger prawns, shell on
400g black linguine (made with squid ink)
1 tablespoon extra-virgin olive oil
120g cured chorizo, chopped into little cubes (not the raw or semi-raw chorizo)
2 Spanish onions, finely chopped (or any yellow or white onion if unavailable)

4 cloves of garlic, peeled and grated superfine
a large pinch of saffron
1 large red chilli, very finely chopped
800g clams
150ml medium dry sherry, such as amontillado
juice of 1 orange
juice of ½ lemon
salt and freshly ground black pepper
2 handfuls of flat-leaf parsley, roughly chopped

Take the head and the shell off the prawns until you reach the tail. Holding on to each tail, run a small sharp knife along the spine of the prawn until you reach the thin intestinal tube, which is either clear or mud coloured. Remove this tube and set the prawns aside as you do them.

Cook the linguine according to the packet instructions (this will take roughly 6 minutes depending on the pasta). Drain, splash a tiny bit of olive oil in the pan to prevent sticking, give it a stir and set aside, covered in clingfilm and a clean tea towel to keep it warm.

In a large (and I mean family-sized) saucepan, heat the olive oil and fry the prawns and chorizo for roughly 5 minutes over a high heat until really golden.

Add the onion, garlic, saffron, half the chilli and the clams to the pan and stir for 2 minutes until the onion has softened. Finally, add the sherry, orange juice and lemon juice and cook, covered with a lid and over a medium heat, for 5 minutes until the clams are all open. Taste and season before adding to the pasta and colouring it in with the parsley and the rest of the chilli.

The black linguine in this recipe is a personal favourite, but you could use plain linguine if you fancied it or can't find squid ink. Do really make sure that you don't overcook the pasta because it will lose some of its beautiful colour as well as becoming flabby and horrible.

Roast rack of venison *hawy*

Game in general, and venison in particular, is as full of flavour as it is lean. This recipe has a great balance of flavours and is so simple that it's a joy to use – it's exactly the sort of food that says 'home' to me. Steaming potatoes is hardly ever done in Britain, but the French love them and they are so much more fluffy and delicious.

serves 4
prep time 10 minutes
cooking time 40 minutes (plus 10 minutes resting time)
311 calories per serving

1 teaspoon olive oil
800g rack of venison (go to the butcher for this)
400g baby new potatoes, scrubbed
350g fine haricot (French) beans, tails trimmed
10g unsalted butter
1 clove of garlic, peeled and finely chopped
2 tablespoons Belazu smoked chilli jelly (or tomato chilli jam
   or blackcurrant jelly)
salt and freshly ground black pepper

tip

You won't be surprised to hear that the ENTIRE success of this recipe relies on really good meat, for which you just can't beat a trip down to the friendly butcher. Go on, nip on over and say hello! Resting the meat is another really important part of cooking tender meat and shouldn't be skipped to save time. Consider that *you* might need a bit of R&R too if you had been roasted at 240°C for 20 minutes ... This time will also ensure that your meat is perfectly cooked.

Preheat the oven to 240°C/fan 220°C.
With the help of a pastry brush (or your hands), rub the olive oil over the surface of the rack. Place on a baking tray lined with foil and cook in the hot oven for about 20 minutes (15 minutes for rare, 20 minutes is good for medium rare and 30 minutes for well done).
Meanwhile, give the potatoes a quick wash under the tap and place into a steamer over a pool of boiling water. Steam the potatoes with the lid on for 15 minutes or until they are soft enough to insert the point of a knife.
Next, place the beans in a pan of boiling water for 2 minutes. Drain, then return to the hot pan with the butter and garlic. Cover and set aside.
When the meat is cooked, place onto a clean board, cover completely with foil and a tea towel and leave to rest for 10 minutes.
While the meat is having a siesta, heat up the smoked chilli jam in a separate pan until it is liquid. Glaze the rack with the melted jam before seasoning and slicing the meat between the bones into chops. Serve with the beans and potatoes.

Lamb and butternut squash tagine

This dish is very comforting and satisfying to make as well as to eat. It involves little effort from you because your hob takes the strain, allowing you to relax with a glass of wine (or should I say a spritzer to save you some calories) while a fabulous dish is being created.

serves 6–8
prep time 20 minutes
cooking time 1 hour 45 minutes
495 calories per serving (serving 6)
371 calories per serving (serving 8)

800g leg of lamb, cut into 3cm pieces
1½ tablespoons olive oil
1 large onion, sliced
2 large cloves of garlic, peeled and crushed
1 teaspoon ground cinnamon
1½ teaspoons cumin seeds
1 teaspoon ground ginger
2 good pinches of saffron
410g tin chickpeas, drained
450ml lamb stock
400g tin plum tomatoes
200g couscous
30g sunflower seeds
2 handfuls of roughly chopped coriander
a handful of roughly chopped mint
550g butternut squash, peeled and cut into 2.5cm chunks
salt and freshly ground black pepper

Brown the lamb in batches in a large, deep non-stick frying pan over a high heat with a tablespoon of the oil. Add a bit of water to the saucepan to deglaze the pan between frying each batch (this little liquid adds even more flavour to the final dish). Set aside.
Add the remaining oil to the pan and fry the onion over a medium heat for 5 minutes until slightly golden, stirring occasionally.
Add the garlic, cinnamon, cumin seeds, ginger and saffron and stir over the heat for 30 seconds to release the aromas of the spices.
Add the meat back into the onion with the chickpeas, stock and tomatoes.

Bring to the boil, then turn down to a gentle boil, cover and cook for 1 hour. Meanwhile, put the couscous into a large bowl. Add the sunflower seeds and a third of the herbs and cover with 200ml cold water. Set aside for the water to be absorbed.

After 1 hour, add the butternut squash and the remaining herbs, apart from about a tablespoon, to the tagine and cook for a further 15 minutes, uncovered. After the 15 minutes has passed, season the tagine well.

Fork through the couscous to separate the grains and spread evenly over the top of the tagine. Cover and simmer for a further 15 minutes.

Serve immediately, ensuring there's some lamb and couscous in each spoonful and sprinkling with the remaining herbs (for the show I presented this by placing a large plate over the casserole dish and inverting it so the couscous was on the bottom with the meat on top. I then lifted the meat to make some height and drizzled with mint yoghurt).

Instead of butternut squash, you could add 100g dried apricots or prunes. And try mixing some shredded mint with 0% fat Greek yoghurt and a little water to make a mint sauce to drizzle over your tagine.

'You can enjoy deliciously comforting food and still drop a dress size.'

Maple-glazed pork with roasted garlic and olive oil mash *sophie*

Okay, so this is a bit of a treat because the maple syrup adds calories, but I've chosen pork fillet because it has very little fat and I've also used olive oil instead of butter for the mash. And don't be put off by the amount of garlic. When you roast garlic, it takes on a beautifully sweet and nutty flavour that combines brilliantly with the silky mash and rich olive oil.

serves 6
prep time 10 minutes
cooking time 1 hour
283 calories per serving

1 large bulb of garlic
3 x 175–200g large potatoes
3 x 200g pork fillets, trimmed
2 tablespoons olive oil
salt and pepper
2 tablespoons maple syrup
2 tablespoons soy sauce
1 sprig of rosemary, chopped

Preheat the oven to 200°C/fan 180°C.
Wrap the unpeeled garlic in foil and roast for about 40 minutes until soft.
While this is cooking, move on to peeling the potatoes. Cut them into equal-sized pieces, cover with cold salted water and bring to the boil. Simmer for about 20 minutes until going soft and cooked through, then drain.
When the garlic is cooked, slice off the top of the bulb carefully with a sharp knife and squeeze the garlic into the potatoes, then mash with the olive oil, salt and pepper.
Mix together the maple syrup, soy sauce and rosemary in a bowl. Coat each pork fillet in this mixture.
Heat up a frying pan until very hot and brown the fillets on each side for about 6 to 8 minutes, really caramelizing them and getting a good colour all over, then finish in the oven for about 5 minutes. The timing will depend on how big the fillets are. Don't overcook them as there is very little fat on a fillet and it can dry out quickly.
Finally, gently heat the mash and serve with slices of the pork about 5 to 8mm thick and some lovely French beans or broccoli.

Teriyaki roast beef with sesame greens and coconut rice *gizzi*

I love roast beef, but it's notoriously fatty. By using fillet, you're cooking with the leanest beef possible. It's expensive, but so worth the results. Fillet really needs to be treated with respect and eaten pink, especially as this is a Japanese-inspired dish.

serves 6–8
prep time 15 minutes
cooking time 60 minutes (plus 15 minutes resting time)
443 calories per serving (serving 6)
590 calories per serving (serving 8)

for the teriyaki sauce
200ml soy sauce
200ml sake (Japanese rice wine)
2 tablespoons mirin (optional)
3 tablespoons fructose sugar

for the beef
900g beef fillet, trimmed and tied (ask your butcher to do this)
salt and freshly ground black pepper
1 tablespoon olive oil
1 tablespoon sesame seeds, (black and white if you can find them)
450g greens (I would use tenderstem broccoli, pak choi or spring greens)
a dash of sesame oil

for the coconut rice
300g basmati rice
400ml tin reduced-fat or light coconut milk
salt

Preheat the oven to 200°C/fan 180°C.
Place all the teriyaki ingredients in a small saucepan and cook over a low heat until the sugar melts. When melted, raise the temperature and boil for 3 to 5 minutes or until the sauce has reduced and is thick and syrupy. Pour into a measuring jug to cool. There should be around 200ml sauce.

Season the beef with salt and pepper, then brown the outside in a hot roasting tray with the olive oil for around 5 minutes.

Line the roasting tray with some foil and pop it with the beef into the oven and roast for 10 minutes. Remove from the oven and baste by brushing on the teriyaki sauce with a pastry brush. Bake for another 10 minutes and baste again. Finish roasting for 5 minutes.

Remove the beef from the oven, cover with foil and leave to rest for 15 minutes. When you're ready to serve, cut into 1cm slices.

For the greens, toast the sesame seeds in a dry frying pan until golden. Bring a pan of salted water to the boil. Add the greens and boil for about 2 minutes until cooked and tender. Drain, then toss through the sesame oil and seeds.

Place the rice in a saucepan and cover with the coconut milk, 150ml water and some salt. Bring to the boil for 8 minutes or until the water has almost all been absorbed. Turn off the heat and set aside for 10 minutes for the rice to fluff up and absorb the rest of the liquid.

To serve, place a large spoonful of rice in the off-centre of a plate and lay some of the greens next to it. Top with a couple of slices of beef and drizzle with a teaspoon of the leftover teriyaki sauce.

tip

If you were pushed for time or ingredients, you could use a ready-made teriyaki sauce. I would buy one from an Asian supermarket though, just to ensure authenticity.

'I've also cooked this with chicken but it only saves a few calories and so I think the stronger, richer flavour of the beef is well worth it.'

Roast rack of lamb with a flageolet bean and artichoke salad *gizzi*

There is something so satisfying about eating lamb. Perhaps it's because it's considered fairly high in fat, but if you get your butcher to trim the racks of lamb, this will reveal delicious lean meat. If you can't find artichokes, then you can replace them with shredded savoy cabbage or kale.

serves 6
prep time 20 minutes
cooking time 45 minutes
574 calories per serving

1 small bulb of garlic, its top sliced off to reveal the cloves
½ teaspoon olive oil
3 racks of lamb, French trimmed and with all the fat cut off
    (allow half a rack per person or 3 ribs each)
salt and freshly ground black pepper
1 tablespoon olive oil
for the salad
1 tablespoon olive oil
1 sprig of rosemary
3 x 400g cans flageolet beans, rinsed and well drained
400g grilled artichoke hearts (either from the deli counter or in a jar)
3 tablespoons low-fat crème fraîche
3 teaspoons Dijon mustard
a handful of mint, chopped
for the gravy
1 heaped teaspoon plain flour
300ml lamb stock (or chicken if you can't find lamb)

Preheat the oven to 180°C/fan 160°C. Pop in the bulb of garlic drizzled with the olive oil and roast for about 30–45 minutes or until quite soft. Meanwhile, season the lamb generously with salt and pepper. Heat the olive oil in a roasting tray and brown the lamb all over for about 5 minutes. Pop in the oven and bake for 15 to 20 minutes. This should give you perfect medium-cooked lamb. Remove from the oven and leave to rest, covered in foil, for 10 minutes.

To make the salad, heat the olive oil in a heavy-based saucepan. Squeeze the roasted garlic out into the pan and add the rosemary. Fry for 1 minute to release the flavours. Pour in the flageolet beans and artichoke hearts and gently cook over a low heat until warmed through. Add the crème fraîche, mustard, mint and some salt and pepper and stir until combined.

For the gravy, after the lamb has rested, remove from the roasting tray and set aside in a warm place. Heat the fat in the tray on the hob and add the flour. Mix together, scraping all the lamby residue off the bottom of the pan. Pour over a little of the stock to make into a paste, then add the stock, bit by bit, until it's all been combined and the gravy is smooth. Transfer to a small pan and bring to the boil, cooking until the gravy has thickened to a syrupy consistency.

Serve each person with a spoonful of the beans topped with three of the cutlets and the sauce moated around the outside. Delicious!

super sides

We all know it's good to fill up on vegetables, but they can be so bland and boring. Thankfully, all it takes is a little culinary flair and flavour to transform the most mundane of ingredients into something stunning. Here are some side dishes you'll want to make the main event.

Chargrilled courgette ribbons *handy*

Frankly, you could eat these straight from the pan – undressed as it were – until you turned into a courgette without putting on an ounce. All the flavour that you could hope for in a vegetable is right here in this recipe and it's so flipping pretty.

serves 2
prep time 5 minutes
cooking time 15 minutes
32 calories per serving

1 large courgette
1 teaspoon extra-virgin olive oil
juice of ½ lemon
salt and freshly ground black pepper

Heat a griddle pan so that it is seriously hot. Using a potato peeler, shave the courgette lengthways. Place the courgette ribbons flat on the smoking-hot pan and cook until you can see chargrill stripes. Remove with some tongs and set aside. Repeat the process until all the ribbons have been chargrilled and look like long, thin, green zebras.

In a bowl, combine the olive oil and lemon juice. Season the ribbons well with salt and freshly ground black pepper before running the dressing all over them.

Chargrilling these ribbons takes longer than you might first think. Saying that though, it's easy enough to do that bit well in advance and dress them at the last minute. It would also be amazing to finish the recipe off with a few courgette flowers if you could lay your hands on some.

Honey-glazed parsnips

One of the most glorious flavours to come out of the mud, parsnips are a firm British favourite. This recipe is so delicious that it feels like a naughty treat, even though it's not.

serves 2
prep time 5 minutes
cooking time 30 minutes
102 calories per serving

2 medium parsnips (250g), peeled and top and tailed
1/4 teaspoon olive oil
2 teaspoons clear honey
salt and freshly ground black pepper
1/2 teaspoon balsamic vinegar

Preheat the oven to 200°C/fan 180°C.
Cut the parsnips into either quarters or halves (depending on how thick they are) and place on a baking tray lined with parchment paper.
Toss the vegetables first in the olive oil, then the honey and crunch over plenty of salt and pepper.
Cook in the oven for 30 minutes until golden and cooked through. It's a good idea to keep an eye on the parsnips and give them a shake halfway through the cooking process as they do like to tan quietly when no one is looking. Coat in the balsamic vinegar just before serving.

'The more vegetables you can add to your diet, the quicker the pounds will drop off. Experiment and find out what you really like.'

'Choose your veg according to the season. All greens are good for you, fantastic when fresh and very low in calories.'

French beans with ginger and sesame *sophie*

A lot of people seem to think that vegetables are boring – well, I love them! When it comes to losing weight they are also a great way to fill you up. There are so many different ways to make them more exciting, but here is one of my favourites. It is super-quick and makes them taste more interesting. These can be served with anything from steamed chicken to stir-fried chilli prawns

serves 2–3 as a side dish
prep time 5 minutes
cooking time 5 minutes
28 calories per serving

250g French beans, trimmed
½ teaspoon sesame oil
1.5cm knob of ginger, peeled and cut into fine slivers
1 teaspoon sesame seeds
2 teaspoons soy sauce

Heat up a large saucepan of water until rapidly boiling. Add salt and quickly put in all the beans. Bring to the boil and simmer for 3 minutes. Drain and run under cold water until chilled, then completely drain, ideally patting dry using a clean tea towel.
Heat up a wok or frying pan and add the oil, then add the ginger and sesame seeds, cook for 1 minute and add the beans. Stir-fry until coated and finally stir in the soy sauce. Then simply serve!

tip

I also stir-fry French beans and broccoli with chilli and garlic using the same method.

Balsamic roasted cherry tomatoes *sophie*

These are great and go with so many different dishes. They are good with steak, on toast, with pasta or even baked with a piece of sea bass – people love them. There are also lots of variations. You can use a mix of yellow and red tomatoes or a sprinkle of thyme instead of basil.

serves 2
prep time 10 minutes
cooking time 15 minutes
51 calories per serving
with one thick slice of granary toast, 181 calories per serving

250g cherry tomatoes
1 clove of garlic, left in its skin and crushed
½ tablespoon olive oil
½ tablespoon balsamic vinegar
sea salt
a handful of shredded basil

Preheat the oven to 200°C/fan 180°C.
Put the tomatoes and garlic in a small roasting tray and toss with the olive oil, vinegar and a sprinkle of the sea salt.
Roast for around 15 minutes or until the tomatoes just begin to soften, but still retain their shape. Take out of the oven, sprinkle with the basil and serve.

Cumin-crusted aubergines

Until recently, aubergines for me were a pointless vegetable that just soaked up oil like a sponge and didn't taste of a lot. However, my opinion has been completely changed by baking them. The flavour is intensified and the flesh is juicy, making them perfect for chopping up and adding to dishes or puréeing into a great dip with some roasted garlic and natural yoghurt. This dish is ideal as an accompaniment to lamb, chicken or barbecued meats.

serves 2
prep time 10 minutes
cooking time 25–30 minutes
69 calories per serving

1 medium aubergine
½ teaspoon cumin seeds
½ teaspoon coriander seeds
1 small shallot, finely chopped
1 small clove of garlic, peeled and finely chopped
¼ teaspoon paprika
½ tablespoon extra-virgin olive oil
salt and freshly ground black pepper
75g 0% fat Greek yoghurt
10 mint leaves, shredded

Preheat the oven to 200°C/fan 180°C.
Cut the aubergine in half lengthways and, using a sharp knife, cut a criss-cross pattern into the flesh as far down as 1cm from the skin. Place on a non-stick baking tray.
Using a pestle and mortar, crush the cumin and coriander seeds until quite finely ground. Mix the seeds with the shallot, garlic, paprika and oil. Using your hands, smear this mixture all over the cut sides of the aubergine and down into the criss-crosses.
Season well and bake on the top shelf of the oven for 25–30 minutes until slightly charred and cooked through.
Meanwhile, mix the yoghurt with the mint, season and serve this with the aubergine.

tip
To make peeling shallots easier, place them in some boiling water and leave for 1 to 2 minutes to loosen the skins.

Colcannon

If it were possible, I would say that this is even tastier and more comforting than normal mash (and it needs less butter). Great as a side dish, but good enough to eat on its own.

serves 2
prep time 10 minutes
cooking time 25 minutes
as a main, 352 calories per serving
as a side, 176 calories per serving

600g potatoes, peeled and chopped
20g butter
120ml skimmed milk
salt and freshly ground black pepper
3 spring onions, thinly sliced
2 cloves of garlic, peeled and crushed
150g spring greens, shredded and left in iced water

Put the potatoes into a pan of cold salted water and bring to the boil. Cover and boil for 15 minutes until soft, then drain. Mash the potatoes with a potato masher until smooth. Add half the butter, the milk and some salt and pepper to taste.

Meanwhile, heat the remaining butter in a wok, add the spring onion and garlic and sauté for 2 to 3 minutes. Throw in the greens that have been drained but not dried and stir-fry for 5 minutes or until the greens have softened. Season to taste.

Stir the greens into the mash, check the seasoning and serve.

Potato skins with salsa and guacamole *gizzi*

This makes a fantastic starter, snack or side dish, but if you wanted to make more of a meal out of it, then add a sprinkling of mature Cheddar cheese (you'll use less if it's strong) and a dollop of half-fat soured cream. This fresh zingy salsa will keep you away from the jar stuff for good.

serves 2 as a starter, snack or side dish
prep time 20 minutes
cooking time 1 hour 30 minutes
248 calories per serving

2 large baking potatoes, about
   175–200g each
olive oil spray
for the guacamole
1 small clove of garlic, peeled
   and grated
1 small red chilli, deseeded and
   finely chopped
1 spring onion, thinly sliced
¼ teaspoon ground cumin
salt
juice of ½ lime
1 medium to large avocado

for the salsa
1 clove of garlic, peeled and grated
1 small to medium red chilli,
   deseeded and finely chopped
5 vine tomatoes, deseeded and
   really finely chopped
juice of 1 lime
a splash of Tabasco
a splash of olive oil
salt and freshly ground black pepper
a handful of finely chopped coriander

Preheat the oven to 180°C/fan 160°C.
Bake the potatoes for 45 to 60 minutes.
To make the salsa, place all the ingredients into a bowl and mix together. For a really strong flavour, leave for an hour.
Remove the potatoes from the oven and, using either a tea towel or oven gloves, carefully cut each potato's skin into thirds, leaving about 5mm of flesh in each as you go. You should end up with three equal-sized potato skins for each potato.
Lay on a baking tray and spritz with olive oil. Bake for a further 20 minutes or until crisp and golden.
To make the guacamole, place the garlic, chilli, spring onion, cumin and salt into a bowl and mix well with the lime juice. Add the avocado and mash with a fork until fairly smooth, but with the odd lump.
Serve the potatoes on a plate with the guacamole and salsa.

Sweet potato gratin *sophie*

I love a big plate of cream and garlic potato gratin but, oh, is it fattening. In my attempts to create a healthier version, this recipe has become quite far removed from the original and has its own identity, but it is, nevertheless, lovely. It works brilliantly with some lime-and-ginger marinated seared salmon and a dollop of low-fat crème fraîche.

serves 8 (I would normally serve half and then freeze the other half)
prep time 15 minutes
cooking time 1 hour
164 calories per serving

6–8 sweet potatoes
3 cloves of garlic, peeled and finely chopped
5cm knob of ginger, peeled and grated
1 red chilli, deseeded and finely chopped
50g butter
salt
a bunch of spring onions, thinly sliced
250ml warm vegetable stock

Preheat the oven to 180°C/fan 160°C.
Peel and slice the sweet potatoes thinly and place them into a large bowl. I use a Japanese mandolin for this, but you can slice them by hand.
Place the garlic, ginger and chilli in a small saucepan with the butter and a good pinch of salt. Melt the butter completely down and pour the mixture into the potatoes with the spring onion.
Take a 25 x 20cm baking or gratin dish and layer the potato mix up, seasoning lightly in between. It will look a bit funny at this point and there will be gaps. Don't worry because as it starts cooking, the potatoes will soften and you can press them down.
Pour over the vegetable stock and bake for around 40 minutes, then turn the heat up to 200°C/fan 180°C for the last 15 minutes and cook until golden on top and cooked through. When you take the gratin out, press down a little to make it more compact and then it is ready to serve.

Shredded savoy cabbage with toasted pine nuts and crispy prosciutto *savoy*

Cabbage is just about the most misunderstood vegetable in the patch. From Charlie Bucket's family huddled around cabbage and boiled potatoes in Roald Dahl's *Charlie and the Chocolate Factory* to the dreaded Cabbage Soup Diet, this old friend has been battered with the ugly stick. This recipe is wonderful, super-simple and puts cabbage back where it should be: green, glorious, and somewhere near the top.

serves 2
prep time 5 minutes
cooking time 15 minutes
150 calories per serving

250g savoy cabbage
20g pine nuts
35g prosciutto
½ teaspoon olive oil
2 sage leaves, finely chopped
salt
¼ teaspoon white pepper

Take the outer leaves off the cabbage from the outside in and, using a sharp knife, remove the core. Roll the leaves up like cigars and slice into thin ribbons. Give them a quick wash under the tap and set aside without bothering to dry them too much.

In a large dry frying pan, toast the pine nuts over a medium-high heat until golden. It's always a good idea with pine nuts not to wander off or get distracted because they catch and burn in the blink of an eye. When toasted and lovely, remove them from the pan and set aside. Next add the prosciutto, laying it out flat in the bottom of the pan for 4 minutes until it has shrunk slightly and gone crispy. Set aside with the pine nuts.

Heat the pan up and pop in the olive oil, sage and cabbage. Stir-fry this mixture for 5 minutes, then put in 1 teaspoon water, turn the heat off completely and place the lid on for another 2 minutes. Season with salt and white pepper, then add the prosciutto in little shards and the pine nuts before serving.

tip

This recipe is awesome with pale flavours like grilled fish or chicken and with just a quick squeeze of lemon over the meat.

Duo-bean salad with an oregano and lemon dressing *sal*

This is one of the dishes that originated from a trip I took to Tuscany with some of my foodie friends, where we all enjoyed using the luscious local ingredients to make dinner. It's made with fresh oregano, which in my opinion is a much underused herb. Hopefully, after making this dish, you will agree it is time to get oregano back on the map.

serves 2
prep time 10 minutes (plus 20 minutes marinating time)
138 calories per serving

125g fine beans, trimmed
1 tablespoon finely chopped fresh oregano leaves
½ small love of garlic, peeled and crushed
zest of ½ lemon
1–1½ tablespoons lemon juice
1 tablespoon extra-virgin olive oil
salt and freshly ground black pepper
200g tinned butter beans, rinsed and drained
100g drained roasted red peppers (from a jar)
½ small red onion, thinly sliced

Bring lots of water to the boil in a large saucepan, add the fine beans, bring back to the boil and boil for 2 minutes. Test one bean to make sure it is cooked but still has some crunch. Immediately plunge the beans into cold water to retain their colour, then drain when cooled.

Whisk together the oregano, garlic, lemon zest and juice with the olive oil, and season well.

Toss the dressing through all the remaining ingredients and check the seasoning. Allow to marinate for 20 minutes and serve with griddled tuna or chicken.

tip

Buy the roasted red peppers in brine rather than oil because they are lower in fat.

Ratatouille

This recipe stands up just as well as a main course as it does a side dish, but it's especially delicious with lamb. By adding a can of red kidney or blackeye beans and 1 tablespoon cumin, you can also change it into a speedy vegetable chilli.

serves 4
prep time 15 minutes
cooking time 45 minutes
154 calories per serving

2 tablespoons olive oil
1 red onion, chopped
1 clove of garlic, peeled and chopped
1 red chilli, deseeded and chopped
1 aubergine, chopped into 1cm cubes
2 courgettes, chopped into 1cm cubes
1 red pepper, deseeded and chopped into 1cm pieces
1 green pepper, deseeded and chopped into 1cm pieces
1 yellow pepper, deseeded and chopped into 1cm pieces
2 x 400g tins chopped tomatoes
2 tablespoons tomato purée
½ teaspoon sugar (or to taste)
a splash of balsamic vinegar
5 sprigs of fresh thyme
salt and freshly ground black pepper

Heat the oil in a large, heavy-based saucepan. Fry the onion, garlic and chilli for 3 to 4 minutes or until they begin to soften. Add the aubergine and fry for 5 to 8 minutes or until it turns a pale golden brown. Add the courgette and peppers and fry for a further 5 to 8 minutes.
Pour over the tomatoes and add the tomato purée, sugar, vinegar and thyme. Season with the salt and pepper. Cook, covered, over a low heat for 10 minutes and then 10 minutes uncovered. It is ready when the ratatouille has thickened slightly.

Thai mango sauce *gizzi*

A delicious, piquant and pretty much fat-free sauce that's great with fish or chicken.

serves 2
prep time 5 minutes
56 calories per serving

1 very ripe mango, peeled and stoned
juice of 1 lime
1 tablespoon fish sauce
1 red chilli, deseeded and roughly chopped
1 small knob of ginger (about 2 teaspoons), peeled and grated
1 small clove of garlic, peeled and grated
a small handful of chopped coriander

Place all the ingredients into a blender and blitz until smooth.

Port and blueberry sauce *sophie*

This is a quick, easy and tasty sauce. I love serving it with duck or venison.

serves 4
prep time 15 minutes
89 calories per serving

150ml of red wine
75ml of Port
100ml a cup of chicken stock
2 handfuls of blueberries
1 tablespoon of redcurrant jelly
salt and pepper

Pour the port and wine into a frying pan, then cook the alcohol off for a couple of minutes. Add the blueberries, redcurrant jelly and the stock and simmer until the liquid is reduced by a third – this should take about 8 to 10 minutes. When the sauce has thickened to a consistency you like, season and serve.

Asian salad dressing *gizzi*

A dressing inspired by the famous Wagamama salad, but with my own stamp on it.
A great alternative to a vinaigrette or creamy dressing.

makes enough for 1 large salad
prep time 15 minutes
35 calories per serving

½ teaspoon wasabi powder
½ small knob of ginger (about 1 teaspoon), peeled and grated
1 small clove of garlic, peeled and grated
1 tablespoon rice wine vinegar
a squeeze of lime juice
1 tablespoon olive oil
1 teaspoon toasted sesame oil

Place all the ingredients in an old jam jar and shake like crazy for 30 seconds.

Salsa verde *harry*

serves 2
prep time 10 minutes
118 calories per serving

a small handful of flat-leaf parsley
a small handful of tarragon
a small handful of basil
1 teaspoon capers
1 small clove of garlic, peeled
1 tablespoon toasted sesame oil (optional)
1 tablespoon extra-virgin olive oil
1 teaspoon tarragon vinegar
1 teaspoon Dijon mustard
salt and freshly ground black pepper

Place all the ingredients in a small blender or pestle and mortar and blitz or pound until well mixed and coarsely chopped. Season to taste.

Mango salsa

serves 2
prep time 15 minutes
39 calories per serving

1 small ripe mango, peeled, stoned and finely chopped
½ small cucumber, peeled, deseeded and finely chopped
¼–½ red chilli, deseeded and finely chopped
¼ small red onion, finely chopped
a handful of roughly chopped coriander
zest of ½ lime
1½–2 tablespoons lime juice
salt and freshly ground black pepper

Stir all the ingredients together and season well. Allow the mixture to marinate for an hour before serving with the spice-crusted salmon on page 124, barbecued chicken or seared tuna.

Ready-made dressings

Average calories per 20g serving
Caesar 83
Blue cheese 64
French 54
Thousand Island 31
Honey mustard 18
Balsamic Italian 16

Dips

Average calories per 100g
Taramasalata 479
Houmus 312
Sourcream & chive 282
Guacamole 185
Tzatziki 126
Salsa 51

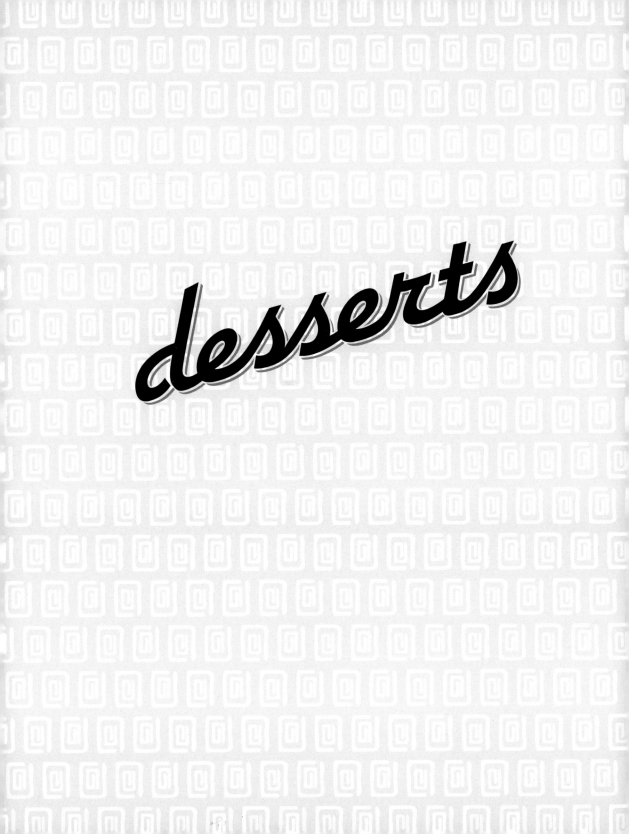

desserts

If you have a sweet tooth then you'll know diet desserts (or, worse, no dessert!) just don't work. That soapy, synthetic-tasting low-cal trifle will have you reaching for the biscuit tin in no time. The key is using good, quality ingredients and maximizing taste, so you don't overdo the portion size. Try it our way and you won't have to miss out.

Chocolate and orange tiramisu

Tiramisu literally translates as 'pick me up'. This pudding will certainly do that with a little alcohol, coffee and chocolate, but it's not a case of 'a moment on the lips and an inch on the hips', more 'have a little sin and still be thin'. If you don't have an orange liqueur, you could try dark rum or amaretto.

serves 6
prep time 15 minutes (plus 30 minutes freezing time
and 1–2 hours setting time)
217 calories per serving

2 ½ tablespoons orange liqueur, Grand Marnier or Cointreau
120ml strong black coffee
20g Maya Gold chocolate (Green & Blacks)
2 large eggs, separated
40g caster sugar
200g light cream cheese
150g 2% fat Greek yoghurt
1 tablespoon cocoa powder, plus extra to dust
12 sponge fingers, halved

You can make the tiramisu the night before. For alternative toppings, you could sprinkle over some unrefined dark muscovado sugar 20 to 30 minutes before serving or a little grated chocolate. If the muscovado sugar is a bit clumped together, heat it in the microwave for 20 to 30 seconds to separate the granules. If you're pregnant (or feeding a baby or elderly person), then do note that this recipe contains raw eggs.

Add 1 ½ tablespoons orange liqueur to the strong coffee and put to one side. Place the chocolate in the freezer for 30 minutes, then finely grate. In a bowl, beat together the egg yolks and caster sugar with an electric mixer for about 2 to 3 minutes until thick and pale.

Whisk in the cream cheese, Greek yoghurt, cocoa powder and the remaining tablespoon of orange liqueur and beat until smooth.

In a separate bowl, beat the egg whites until stiff peaks form with a balloon whisk or electric mixer. Fold the egg whites gently into the yoghurt mixture.

Dip half the sponge fingers into the coffee liqueur mixture for about 2 seconds on each side and shake off the excess. Cover the bottom of six individual 200ml dessert glasses.

Sprinkle over half of the chocolate and then spread half of the yoghurt mixture over the chocolate. Repeat the process again, using up the biscuits and chocolate and finishing with a chocolate yoghurt layer. Cover the tiramisu with clingfilm and refrigerate for at least 1 to 2 hours until set. The flavours will develop the longer they are left. Dust lightly with cocoa powder and serve.

Lemon meringue mess *harvey*

Lemon meringue pie is a British classic and rightly so. Apart from looking stunning with all that swirling cloud on top, it combines contrasting flavours and textures. Although this recipe omits the pastry, you will find that the crunch of the meringue, the softness of the cream and the sharp ouch of the lemon is all that this dessert needs.

serves 6
prep time 15 minutes
cooking time 2 hours 20 minutes
266 calories per serving

for the meringue
2 free-range egg whites
115g caster sugar
for the lemon curd
2 level tablespoons cornflour
100g golden caster sugar
juice of 5 lemons and the zest of 2
2 free-range egg yolks
for the last bit of white fluff
120ml whipping cream

tip
Meringues keep really well for a couple of days in an airtight container or tin if you wanted to make them ahead. If you don't fancy spending the time making the meringue, you can always buy it and save yourself the hassle, but make sure that you spend the money on good-quality bought meringue as opposed to that white chalk that sets your teeth on edge. If you're pregnant (or feeding a baby or an elderly person), then do note that this recipe contains raw eggs.

Preheat the oven to 120°C/fan 100°C.
First, make the meringue by whipping the egg whites with a handheld whisk until quite stiff, then gradually whisk in the sugar, a tablespoon at a time. Once you are satisfied that you have a feminine and glossy-looking mixture, dollop six blobs onto a baking tray lined with greaseproof paper and pop into the oven for 2 hours.
To make the lemon curd, put the cornflour, sugar, lemon juice (strain this in with a sieve to prevent lumps later) and the lemon zest into a small saucepan over a medium heat. Stir for roughly 7 minutes until thickened. Take the pan off the heat for 5 minutes in order to cool slightly. Beat in the egg yolks with a balloon whisk until combined and set aside.
Whip the cream with a handheld whisk until soft but not stiff.
To assemble, roughly crunch up the meringue so that you have a mixture of different-sized chunks and textures. Gently fold most of the lemon curd, followed by all the cream (this is important to create the ripple effect) into the meringue before dividing the mess up. Finish off by running the remaining curd in swirly whirlies over the mixture in the bowls. You could garnish with some lemon zest or a spot of mint to smarten it up a notch.

Banoffee pie pots *gizzi*

This is pretty much a storecupboard pudding and investing in a jar of dulce de leche, which you can find at most big supermarkets, will mean you can create this pud in minutes. I'm going to be bold and say this version is better than its full-fat sibling.

serves 2
prep time 5 mins
289 calories per serving

1 large oat or ginger biscuit (about 25g)
2 heaped tablespoons dulce de leche
1 banana, sliced
2½ tablespoons 0% fat Greek yoghurt
chocolate, for grating

Place the biscuit in a plastic bag or pestle and mortar and smash it until it resembles breadcrumbs. Split between two ramekins or small bowls. Top each with 1 tablespoon dulce de leche. This is VERY sticky so be patient, but the great thing is that it doesn't need to be that neat. Lay the banana slices on top and spoon over the yoghurt. Finish by covering the yoghurt with finely grated chocolate.

Strawberry and honey cream tart *sophie*

This is a wonderful summer dessert recipe that I've changed around because it traditionally had a sweet pastry base containing lots of butter and eggs. Pastry can also be a bit of a pain to make, so I have done a quick, easy base with crushed digestive biscuits. The filling is usually crème pâtissière (lovely, but again, sugar, milk, eggs and flour) so I've made a filling out of low-fat cream cheese and my favourite natural sweetener – honey.

serves 10
prep time 15 minutes (plus 1–2 hours chilling time)
314 calories per serving

250g digestive biscuits
100g unsalted butter
500g light cream cheese
3 tablespoons honey
1 vanilla pod, cut in half lengthways and seeds scraped out
2 x 227g punnets of strawberries, hulled
150g punnet of blueberries
icing sugar, for dusting

Blitz the biscuits in a blender until fine. Melt the butter and mix in with the biscuits, then press into the base and sides of a shallow 25 x 26cm loose-bottomed tart tin, pop into the fridge and start on the filling.
Whip the cream cheese with the honey and vanilla seeds and spread into the tart case with the back of a damp spoon. Sometimes the consistency of cream cheese can vary, so if it seems a bit runny, leave in the fridge for a few hours to set.
Halve the strawberries and arrange beautifully over the filling. Finally, sprinkle with blueberries and dust with icing sugar. Chill for around 1 hour before serving.

tip
You also can use different types of fruit – figs are great or even just raspberries.

Chocolate truffles *havey*

The minute that you mention the 'c' word, everyone takes a sharp intake of breath and starts tut-tutting as if you're about to commit a crime! This recipe is different from most truffle recipes because it doesn't contain any cream, butter or anything else white that might dilute the flavour of the chocolate. These truffles are perfect for presents, for after-dinner bits and bobs or for when you just fancy a little chocolate HIT.

makes 24 truffles
prep time 30 minutes (plus 30 minutes chilling time)
cooking time 5 minutes
53 calories per truffle

200g good-quality dark chocolate (70% cocoa solids is good)
6 tablespoons strong black coffee (such as espresso)
2 tablespoons clear honey, such as acacia (nothing with too
    strong a flavour)
cocoa powder, to dust

Melt your chocolate gently in a large bowl over a pan of simmering water before removing it and setting aside. At this stage, it should appear like a liquid pool of chocolate. Gently (it's always best to be gentle with this *most* delicate friend) pour in the coffee and, using a spatula, give it a slow turn of the bowl until the consistency thickens. The texture of the chocolate will start to seize and thicken almost instantly.

Add the honey, a tablespoon at a time, slowly waltzing the chocolate around the bowl until you get a highly glossy lick of chocolate. The whole process will not take more than a couple of minutes.

Chill the bowl in the fridge for 30 minutes or until the truffle mixture has returned to a nearly solid form.

Prepare a clean surface on which to roll out the truffles and sieve 3 generous tablespoons cocoa powder onto it. Scrape out a teaspoonful of the mixture into the palm of your hand and roll into a marble-sized ball, then roll this through the cocoa powder until fully coated and pop into a bowl or jar. Repeat the process until all the mixture is used up and store the little marbles of wonder in the fridge.

tip

You could easily flavour the truffles either with booze (I like Champagne or Vin Santo) or with herbs such as rosemary, cardamom or saffron. Simply make up a tea using 150ml boiling water and a good pinch of the chosen herb (having bashed it up vigorously in a pestle and mortar first to release the flavour). Let the 'tea' infuse for 15 minutes and replace the coffee in this recipe with 6 tablespoons of your own strong, home-made herb tea. Alternatively, replace the coffee with the chosen alcohol, taking care that it is at room temperature or you will upset the chocolate.

Beetroot chocolate fudge cake *hayc*

This beetroot chocolate fudge cake will hit you between the eyes and knock you out. The beauty of this recipe is that it is incredibly rich and deep in flavour, yet uses hardly any flour or fat. I promise you that a little will go a long way. The beetroot is not a touch of madness, it actually provides the gungy texture that makes a great fudge cake and some natural pink sweetness too.

serves 16
prep time 30 minutes
cooking time 2 hours
305 calories per slice

250g good-quality dark chocolate
3 medium free-range eggs
250g light muscovado sugar
1 vanilla pod, cut in half lengthways
    and seeds scraped out
2 tablespoons maple syrup
2 tablespoons clear honey
40g self-raising flour
40g plain flour
1/4 teaspoon bicarbonate of soda
1/4 teaspoon salt

25g cocoa powder
50g ground almonds
250g raw beetroot, peeled and
    finely grated
100ml strong black coffee
30 ml sunflower oil
for the topping
150g good-quality dark chocolate
3 tablespoons strong black coffee
1 teaspoon vanilla essence
3 tablespoons clear honey

tip

Leave yourself plenty
of time to make this
cake because it is quite
a lengthy recipe. The
cake is best eaten
when it is still slightly
warm and it is also
really important to ice
it at the last minute or
the icing can lose its
shine. However, it
would freeze beautifully
providing you put it
away before icing.
Simply defrost when
needed and ice at the
last minute.

Preheat the oven to 160°C/fan 140°C.
With the help of a brush and a tiny bit of sunflower oil, grease the surface
of a round 20cm diameter x 8cm high loose-bottomed tin and set aside.
Melt the chocolate gently in a bowl over a pan of simmering water until
all dissolved, then set aside to cool. In a large mixing bowl, beat the eggs
with the sugar, the scraped-out vanilla seeds, the maple syrup and the
honey for 3 minutes with an electric hand whisk until pale and quite fluffy.
Gently fold in the flours, bicarbonate of soda, salt, cocoa and ground
almonds until fully incorporated.
Using some kitchen paper, dab the grated beetroot thoroughly to remove
some of the excess moisture. Fold in the beetroot, cooled chocolate, coffee
and oil with the help of a spatula until thoroughly mixed together.
Pour the mixture into the prepared tin and cook in the middle of the oven
for 1 hour 30 minutes. After this time, cover the cake with foil and bake for
another 30 minutes. Test the cake by inserting a skewer into the centre to
see if it comes out clean (although this cake is so moist that even when the
cake is fully cooked, the skewer comes out looking *slightly* messy). Leave
to cool on a wire rack.
To make the fudge topping, melt the chocolate gently in a bowl over a
pan of simmering water, then remove from heat and add the coffee and
the vanilla essence. At this stage the chocolate will seize up slightly, but
it will relax back once you add the honey and gently mix in. Set aside
to cool for 15 minutes before icing the cake. Cut the cake through the
middle and ice it in the centre and on all sides.
Decorate the top with whatever you fancy, but I like using pink flowers, such
as tulips or roses, which I plant into the cake with a bit of stem left on.

Lime and ginger fruit platter *sal*

Everyone loves a fruit salad, but often you associate it with being on a diet. To ring the changes, jazz the fruit up with a little warmth from stem ginger and the zestiness of some limes. Also, chop the fruit into quite large pieces and serve on a platter all higgledy-piggledy rather than in a bowl.

serves 6
prep time 10 minutes (plus 30 minutes marinating time)
cooking time 5 minutes
134 calories per serving

90g unrefined caster sugar
30g stem ginger, finely chopped
zest of 1 lime
1½ tablespoons lime juice
½ small pineapple, topped and tailed, skinned, cored
    and cut into eighths
2 kiwis, peeled and cut into quarters
100g blueberries
1 small mango, peeled, stoned and cut into large slices
200g strawberries, halved
100g raspberries

Add the caster sugar and the stem ginger to a saucepan with 125ml water and stir over a gentle heat to dissolve. Bring to the boil and boil for 5 minutes until syrupy.
Remove from the heat and stir in the lime zest and juice and allow to cool.
Pour over the fruit and toss gently, leaving at room temperature for at least 30 minutes for the flavours to meld together.
Serve on a large platter all higgledy-piggledy, some pieces of fruit standing to give height and others dotted around.

tip

The fruits can be varied as long as there is a good mix of colours and textures. If you are very short on time, just drizzle the fruit with a little elderflower cordial and some shredded fresh mint. Great served with a good dollop of Greek yoghurt.

Instant raspberry frozen yoghurt *sal*

One of my favourite desserts is a good home-made vanilla ice cream with warm dark chocolate sauce, which is, of course, fine once in a while. This recipe is packed with flavour, but contains less fat and satisfies any urge for indulgence in no time at all.

serves 6
prep time 5 minutes
87 calories per serving

340g frozen raspberries
350g low-fat natural yoghurt (organic would be best)
4 tablespoons unrefined icing sugar
10-year-old balsamic vinegar

In a food processor, pulse together the raspberries, yoghurt and icing sugar until roughly combined.
Serve immediately with ¼ to ½ tablespoon balsamic vinegar drizzled over the top of each serving.

tip

Instead of raspberries, the recipe also works well with frozen mango pieces and a little lime zest instead of the balsamic to bring out the flavour of the fruit.

Blood orange salad with Greek yoghurt and fennel biscotti *sophie*

Puddings are in general something to avoid when trying to lose weight, but this one is very low in fat and high in vitamin C. Biscotti are dry Italian biscuits, which are perfect dipped in coffee, ice cream or any other creamy puddings. I always make a big batch and keep them on hand for guests.

serves 4 (it makes 25–30 biscotti)
prep time 15 minutes
cooking time 30 minutes
Blood orange salad, 188 calories per serving
86 calories per biscotti

4 blood oranges (or normal oranges)
4 normal oranges
400g 0% fat Greek yoghurt
1 tablespoon runny honey
1 teaspoon orange blossom water

for the biscotti
150g shelled whole almonds
10–15g fennel seeds
250g plain flour
a generous pinch of baking powder
150g caster sugar
3 medium free-range eggs

Preheat the oven to 180°C/fan 160°C.
Tip all the ingredients except the eggs into an electric mixer and mix together. Mix the eggs together, stir through the flour and nut mixture and shape into a large, flat log about 30cm long, 12cm wide and 2cm high. Put it onto a baking tray and bake for around 20 minutes or until cooked through, but not too brown.
When cool enough to handle, lift the log onto a board and slice very thinly diagonally. Place the biscuits onto one or two baking trays and bake for another 10 minutes or until pale brown and crisp.
Now for the salad. Cut the tops and bottoms off the oranges, then, with a sharp knife, cut down the sides to remove the skin and pith. Slice the orange into discs and arrange prettily onto individual plates or a platter. Mix the yoghurt with the honey and orange blossom water. Simply serve the oranges with a big dollop of yoghurt and the biscuits. The biscotti keep for about a week and are also great served with coffee.

tip
You can use any nut in the biscotti – pistachios are very cute or even roughly chopped hazelnuts with a little bit of dark chocolate.

drinks

Trendy coffees, cool cocktails, fizzy drinks – even so-called healthy juices – can all be deceptively high in calories. If you indulge regularly, that could well explain the surplus half stone you can never shift. Switch to our alternatives and it'll be gone before you can say, 'Next round please, barman.'

Elderflower iced tea *gizzi*

This is such a light and glamorous cocktail that's it's easy to drink . . . so be careful and have fun.

serves 1
119 calories per serving

ice
a sprig of redcurrants
1½ tablespoons gin
1 tablespoon elderflower cordial
a few splashes of Angostura bitters
Prosecco (100 ml)

Use thawed frozen redcurrants if you can't get hold of any fresh ones.

Place the ice and redcurrants into a tall glass. Pour over the gin, elderflower cordial and bitters, then fill the glass to the top with Prosecco. Stir and serve.

Mandarin Bellinis *sophie*

Bellinis originated at the Hotel Cipriani in Venice. I love the Cipriani restaurants and they have them all over the world now. The original is made with peach, but this version is less sweet and uses mandarins. It's very aromatic and works beautifully.

serves 1
82 calories per serving

1 part freshly squeezed mandarin juice (juice your own mandarins always)
3 parts Champagne (use Ultra Brut Champagne or chilled dry Prosecco)

When mandarins are out of season, use fresh orange juice.

Mix together. Drink!

Spiced hot chocolate *sal*

By frothing the milk using a cafetiere, you get all the indulgence but with less fat because you're using semi-skimmed milk and less of it. It's perfect for making cappuccinos, lattes and hot chocolates without needing to walk out the front door to get your fix from a coffee shop.

serves 2
prep time 2 minutes
cooking time 2–3 minutes
140 calories per serving

500ml semi-skimmed milk
2 whole star anise
2 cinnamon sticks
2 teaspoons unrefined caster sugar
3 level teaspoons cocoa powder, sifted, plus extra for serving

Put 450ml of the milk, the star anise and the cinnamon in a non-stick saucepan and bring to the boil, being careful it doesn't boil over. Meanwhile, divide the sugar, cocoa powder and the remaining 50ml milk between two mugs and mix thoroughly using a teaspoon.
Remove the star anise and cinnamon from the hot milk and pour into a large cafetiere. Pull the plunger up and down for about 15 to 25 seconds to froth the milk.
Pour into the two mugs, stirring continuously. Using a spoon, top with any remaining froth from the bottom of the cafetiere, sift over a little bit of cocoa powder and serve immediately.

tip
To increase the cinnamon flavour, use a cinnamon stick as a stirrer.

Passion fruit Margarita *gizzi*

I love Margaritas but sometimes they just don't have enough of that mouth puckering sourness which gives them their edge. By adding passion fruit to the mix you get a fuller bodied roundness to the finished result and they are far more 'girl friendly' and drinkable.

serves 1
prep time 5 mins
95 calories per serving

4–5 ice cubes
1 measure tequilla
1 measure lime juice
½ measure Cointreux
the sieved juice of 2 passion fruits
salt
slices of passion fruit

Dampen the edge of half a Margarita glass with some lime juice, and then dip into some fine salt to crystallise.
Place the iced cubes into a cocktail shaker, adding the tequila, lime juice, Cointreux and passion fruit juice. Shake for 30 seconds. Strain into the glass and decorate by placing a round of passion fruit into the glass.

Pomegranate and mint martini *sophie*

Now, we can't be angels all the time, so when you feel your 'halo' slipping and a hand reaching for a sugary alcoholic drink, reach for this instead. Obviously it's better to not drink at all, but that ain't happening in my camp, so here is a brilliant lower-calorie drink. This is also a kind of de-tox while you re-tox. Pomegranate is full of antioxidants and goodness, so I console myself that although it's a little naughty, it's not half as bad as some of the drinks I could be having.

serves 2
113 calories per serving

1 part vodka
3 parts 100% natural pomegranate juice (you can get this in most supermarkets now, but try and avoid ones with added sugars. POM Wonderful is a great make)
crushed ice cubes
3 sprigs of mint
1 pomegranate (this is for the seeds, you need about a tablespoon per cocktail. You can also buy the seeds ready picked in most supermarkets)

Measure the vodka and juice into a cocktail shaker. Add a small handful of ice and 2 sprigs of the mint. Put the cocktail lid firmly back on and shake it like a pro!
Take two martini glasses and add a spoonful of pomegranate seeds to each one. Strain in the vodka mix, not letting the ice go in, and finish with a little mint leaf. These are quite potent, so drink in moderation!

calorie counter

Quick calorie guide

The following is a basic guide to the calorie counts of common foods. We're not for one second suggesting you become a calorie bore, but it's here to help you design your own recipe combinations. You don't have to become a slave to calories, but you can take charge of your own waistline.

FRUIT AND VEG

Apple (1) 50
Apricot (1) 19
    (and dried) 20g/240
Artichoke hearts half can/35
Asparagus 5 spears,
    (cooked) 33
Aubergine 18
Banana 90
Beansprouts 50g/13
Beetroot 9
Blueberries 150g/66
Broccoli 90g/22
Butternut squash 28g/9
Cabbage 90g/14
Carrot 28g/6
Cauliflower 28g/8
Celeriac 28g/4
Celery 1 stalk/3
Cherries 28g/14
Corn on the cob 75g/44
Courgette 28g/5
Cranberries 28g/4
    (and dried) 10g/34
Cucumber 14g/1
Dates (1 dried) 54
Fennel 28g/3
Fig 16
    (and dried) 32
French beans 28g/7
Gherkin 5
Grapefruit 68
Grapes 80g/50
Honeydew melon 28g/8
Kale 28g/7
Kiwi fruit 25
Leeks 28g/6
Lettuce 28g/4
Lychees 28g/16 (19 if in
    syrup)

Mandarin (1 raw) 18
    (tinned in juice) 28g/11
Mango 114
Mushrooms 28g/3
Nectarine 53
Olives in brine (black) 25g/51
    (green) 25g/38
Onions 28g/6
Orange 59
Papaya 28g/8
Parsnip (cooked) 28g/18
Peach 28g/9
Pear 78
Peas 75g/51
Peppers 28g/7
Pineapple (fresh) 200g/99
    (tinned in syrup) 240g/158
Plum 32
Potatoes (boiled) 120g/86
Prunes 50g/79
Pumpkin 28g/4
Radish 28g/3
Raspberries 28g/7
Rhubarb 28g/2
Rocket 50g/10
Satsuma 21
Spinach 28g/7
Spring onions 28g/7
Strawberries 28g/8
Sweet potato 28g/24
Sweetcorn 28g/31
Tomato 85g/15
Watermelon 250g/75

RICE, PASTA AND PULSES

American long grain white
    rice 50g/175
Baked beans 400g can/346
Brown basmati rice 50g/177
Brown rice 75g/267
Cous cous 50g/178
Egg noodles 28g/109
Pasta 100g/352
Polenta 65g/232
Popcorn (popped in
    saucepan, no
    butter/salt/sugar) 74g/282
Rice noodles 30g/110
Risotto (Arborio) rice
    80g/279
Thai rice 50g/174
White basmati rice 60g/212
Wholewheat pasta 100g/324

CEREAL AND BREAD PRODUCTS

All Bran 40g/112
Bagel 78g/215
Baguette 60g/144
Branflakes 30g/99
Ciabatta 73g/174
Cornflakes 30g/112
Cracker bread 19
Cream cracker 34
Croissant (small) 180
Crumpet 80
Foccacia 47g/131
Medium slice brown bread 74
Medium slice Granary bread 83
Medium slice white bread 93
Medium slice wholegrain bread 78
Muesli 40g/144
Naan bread 160g/538
Oatcake 47
Pain au chocolate 235
Pitta 75g/199
Porridge 40g/145 (not incl. milk)
Rice cake 27
Rice Krispies 30g/114
Rye bread 25g/55
Shredded Wheat (2 pieces) 149
Special K 30g/112
Waffle 127
Water biscuits (1 biscuit) 35
Weetabix (2 pieces) 117
Wholemeal bagel 85g/187

NUTS AND SEEDS

Almonds 20g/122
Brazil nuts (6 nuts) 137
Cashews 25g/146
Dry-roasted peanuts 20g/117
Pine nuts 28g/195
Pistachios 15g/92
Pumpkin seeds tbsp/57
Roasted, salted peanuts 28g/181
Sunflower seeds tbsp/59

DAIRY

Clotted cream 100g/579
Cottage cheese 28g/29 (low fat) 28g/22
Crème fraîche 100g/362 (half fat) 100g/181
Double cream 100g/438
Fromage frais 28g/32
Goat's cheese 10g/26
Greek yoghurt 28g/36
Hard cheese 30g/123
Natural yoghurt 100g/80 (fat free) 100g/60
Semi-skimmed milk 200ml/98
Single cream 100g/123
Skimmed milk 200ml/68
Soft cheese 30g/62
Soya milk 200ml/68
Whole milk 200ml/134

MEAT, FISH, EGGS

Bacon (1 rasher) 77
Beef (1 slice roasted) 48 (fillet steak) 28g/54
Chicken 28g/42
Chorizo 80g/250
Duck 28g/48
Egg 82
Ham 50g/57
Lamb (leg) 28g/58
Lobster 28g/29
Parma ham 10g/21
Pork 28g/42
Prawns 28g/21
Quorn (pieces) 300g/309
Salami (slice) 18
Salmon 79g/149
Sardines 28g/55 (canned in tomato sauce) 28g/45
Scallops 10g/8
Skate 28g/18
Swordfish 28g/42
Tofu 100g/119
Trout 120g/159
Tuna 140g/185 (canned in water) 130g/140 (canned in oil) 138g/260
Turkey 28g/33
White fish (cod, haddock, plaice) 28g/25

FATS AND OILS

Butter 7g (a thin
  spreading) 51
Ghee 28g/251
Lard 28g/249
Low-fat cooking spray
  (1 spray) 1
Low-fat spread 7g/25
Margarine 7g/51
Olive oil tbsp/127
Olive-oil spread 10g/56
Sunflower oil tbsp/130
Toasted sesame oil tbsp/45

DRINKS

Alcopops 150–185
Brandy 25ml/52
Cappuccino 110
  (skimmed milk) 60
Champagne 120ml/89
Cider 1pt/205
Cola 330ml/135
Fruit juice 100ml/40–55
Fruit smoothie 100ml/50
Fruit cordial 20ml/20–30
Guinness 1pt/210
Hot chocolate 330
Lager 1pt/165
Latte 260
  (skimmed milk) 160
Port 50ml/79
Red wine 120ml/80
Sherry (dry) 50ml/58
  (sweet) 50ml/68
Tomato/vegetable juice
  100ml/20
Vodka 25ml/52
Whiskey 25ml/52
White wine (dry) 120ml/77

CONDIMENTS

Brown sauce tsp/6
Caesar dressing tbsp/72
Chocolate spread tsp/68
Chutney tsp/25
Coleslaw 28g/72
Custard 28g/119
French dressing tbsp/71
Honey 20g/62
Houmous 50g/150
Jam tsp/25
Ketchup tsp/6
Marmalade tsp/26
Mayonnaise tsp/80
Pesto 28g/142
Salad cream tsp/17
Tahini tsp/115
Taramasalata 85g/407
Thousand Island dressing
  tsp/19
Tzatziki 28g/18

SWEET SNACKS

Carrot cake 46g/156
Cheesecake 28g/119
Chocolate bar (milk) 28g/146
Chocolate cake 28g/128
Chocolate digestive 84
Cream slice 310
Croissant (small) 180
Currant bun 178
Danish pastry 411
Digestive 66
Ice cream (vanilla) 72g/145
Jam doughnut 252
Meringue 8g/30
Muffin 161
Ring doughnut 238
Scone 145
  (fruit scone) 126
Sponge cake with jam
  65g/196

READY MEALS AND SAVOURY SNACKS

Bread stick 20
Cornish pastie 627
Crisps 28g/148
Garlic baguette 60g/187
Pizza (cheese and tomato)
  28g/66
Poppadums 28g/103
Quiche Lorraine 28g/100
Sausage roll 100g/360
Spring roll (vegetable)
  60g/100
Spring roll (chicken) 60g/118
Tortilla chips 50g/240
Vegetable samosa 28g/61
Yorkshire pudding 28g/58

Index

Acknowledgements

A big thank you goes to Camilla, Kate and George at Penguin for their patience and enthusiasm throughout this project. And many thanks to Yuki for her beautiful photographs and to Kim for her very stylish styling. None of this would have been possible without the genius of Jo McGrath, and the never ending kindness of Jenny Freilich – not to mention the rest of the brilliant team at Tiger Aspect. Rebecca, you are wonderful. Harry, Gizzi, Sal and Sophie

Firstly a huge thanks to the other girls, Harry, Sophie and Gizzi for so much fun and laughter, it's been an absolute pleasure working with you all. A massive thanks for the unwavering love and support of my Mum and Dad, my amazing sis Carol, and my two dear brothers Jimbob and Nigs, and in memory of my other brother, Duncan, who I sadly never got to meet but who is often in my thoughts. And of course my 8 nieces and nephews who keep me young and are becoming keen cooks, much to my delight! My career has been shaped by the inspiration, belief and encouragement of Eunice Watson, Tony and Jo Boyle, Roz Denny and Helen White – much love and thanks to you all, not forgetting Guy Lipscombe and Matt Winn for friendship and advice. Finally, life would be boring without the love of food, so thanks to the Supper Club girls who share that passion – I look forward to more nights of gourmandising Sal

I would like to thank my delicious boyfriend, Dean, for putting up with my temporary psychosis while making this book. My mother (my biggest inspiration) has taught me so much and I will continue to strive to be as fantastic a chef as she is. My sisters Heni and Cora, and also Debra, Matt and Edie; you have been my escape from the mayhem. Thank you for putting up with my constant grilling for approval for my recipes. Julia, my agent and friend, thank you for your amazing advice and always being there for me to turn to. Gizzi

My first thanks goes to my Favourite Person, Pie (real name Georgie), for being the best sister, *copine*, flatmate and rock that anyone could hope for. I also want to mention the long chats, great advice and lovely words of friends like Polly, Lucy and Bells . . . Thanks to Martin and the boys at Wyndham House for beautiful, happy meat. Thank you to Rosemary at PFD for your time and encouragement. Finally, thank you to 'the girls', for making this *such* a fun and foodie adventure! Harry

I just want to say a special thank you to my parents, Christina and John Heath, and to my grandparents, Ruth and Edward Hughes, for your never ending support. Sophie

Tiger Aspect would like to thank Harry, Sophie, Sal and Gizzi – we're delighted to have found such varied, talented and charismatic cooks. Thank you for trusting us. Sue Murphy and Walter Iuzzolino at C4 always believed in this idea and constantly improved it. Huge thanks to Hannah Ebelthite, a very talented writer and Lynne Garton, a clever and patient nutritionist. Thank you Jenny Freilich, Rebecca Mulraine, Gordon Wise, Jamie Munro and Jenny Spearing – it's a privilege to work alongside you. Finally, thanks to everyone at Penguin and Smith & Gilmour, particularly Kate Adams and Camilla Stoddart – you're a formidable team. Jo McGrath, Executive Producer